Perfect Personality Profiles

Helen Baron is a Chartered Psychologist who has spent her career researching and developing psychometric tests. An active member of the British Psychological Society, she was a founder member of its Standing Committee for the Promotion of Equal Opportunities and is currently a member of its Standing Committee on Test Standards. She lives in central London.

Other titles in the *Perfect* series

Perfect Answers to Interview Questions, Max Eggert
Perfect Babies' Names, Rosalind Fergusson
Perfect Best Man, George Davidson
Perfect CV, Max Eggert
Perfect Interview, Max Eggert
Perfect Numerical Test Results, Joanna Moutafi and Ian Newcombe
Perfect Psychometric Test Results, Joanna Moutafi and Ian Newcombe
Perfect Pub Quiz, David Pickering
Perfect Punctuation, Stephen Curtis
Perfect Readings for Weddings, Jonathan Law
Perfect Wedding Speeches and Toasts, George Davidson

Perfect
Personality
Profiles

Helen Baron

BOOKS

Published by Random House Books 2007

2 4 6 8 10 9 7 5 3 1

Copyright © Helen Baron 2007

First published in the United Kingdom in 2007 by
Random House Books

Random House Books
Random House, 20 Vauxhall Bridge Road,
London SW1V 2SA

www.randomhouse.co.uk

Addresses for companies within The Random House Group Limited
can be found at: www.randomhouse.co.uk/offices.htm

The Random House Group Limited Reg. No. 954009

A CIP catalogue record for this book
is available from the British Library

ISBN 9781905211821

The Random House Group Limited makes every effort to ensure that the
papers used in its books are made from trees that have been legally sourced
from well-managed and credibly certified forests. Our paper procurement
policy can be found at: www.randomhouse.co.uk/paper.htm

Typeset by Palimpsest Book Production Limited, Grangemouth, Stirlingshire
Printed and bound in Great Britain by CPI Bookmarque, Croydon CR0 4TD

Contents

Introduction

You may be looking at this book because you think you, or someone you know, might have to complete a personality questionnaire in the near future, or perhaps you have filled one in recently. The purpose of this book is to help you understand more about personality questionnaires and the profiles they produce. As with much of what psychologists do, there are some myths and misunderstandings about questionnaires. Some people think they have some magic power to unearth deep secrets about them, while others believe they are all nonsense and are no more valid than horoscopes or tarot cards.

The reality is that psychologists apply scientific methods to thinking about human behaviour. They develop personality questionnaires and profiles as tools to provide descriptions of how individuals behave, and they aim to do this in the most straightforward way that is effective. For the most part there is no magic about the way personality questionnaires work. They ask a series of often very simple questions about how you think, feel and behave and then collate the answers in a standardized way. At their most basic, questionnaires ask you whether you like being with people and then feed back as a result whatever you said.

If questionnaires are so simple why do employers use them so much? Test publishing is a multi-million pound industry in Britain, and as someone who works in the field of test development I am constantly being contacted by new clients who would like me to help them develop another questionnaire. The reason people want psychologists to develop tests and questionnaires for them is that there is a lot of evidence that such measures are more efficient, effective and accurate than most other methods of assessing people. Psychologists have researched the most important factors in understanding people and encapsulated these into questionnaires. This is good for the employers, who can quickly gain a clear and objective picture of an individual. Personality profiles provide accurate, easily comparable information about each applicant for a job.

Questionnaires also benefit candidates and others being tested. The process of being tested is relatively quick and painless. Some questionnaires take up to an hour to complete, but they usually take much less time. More importantly, they produce objective and accurate information that is not subject to the individual biases of an interviewer. Your results won't be different if you have ginger hair or speak with an accent.

In this book I describe what personality is and how it is measured. There is a section on some commonly measured personality traits and characteristics, and this includes some concepts that are related to personality and that you might encounter in questionnaire-based assessments such as competencies and emotional intelligence. You can use this chapter to think about yourself and understand more about your own personality.

This book does not contain a full questionnaire for you to complete. It is not possible to do this effectively because of the variety of needs and backgrounds that readers may have. A full questionnaire is likely to be misleading for at least some people. There is, however, a section with lots of examples of different types of questions so that you can see what questionnaires are like if you have never completed one before and would like to practise answering questions. There is also a section describing how employers might use your questionnaire results.

The chapter on preparation is more about how you don't really need to do much preparation to complete a questionnaire. After all, you are probably quite an expert on the subject of yourself, and what you are being asked to do is describe yourself. However, there are some hints and tips about answering questions and getting the best out of the experience.

At the end of the book are sections on standards in using questionnaires and answers to some frequently asked questions.

I hope the book will help you understand more about personality questionnaires and what they do and, if you are anxious about completing one, that it will allay your fears. Undergoing assessment for any reason, whether you are applying for a job or being assessed to help your development, can be unnerving. The best of us can worry that we won't come up to scratch or will be found wanting.

Although the book is called *Perfect Personality Profiles* there are no 'good' or 'bad' personalities. It isn't better to be extrovert than introvert or flexible than structured. These are just different ways of being. Of course, some personalities are better suited than others to some roles: sales people need to be outgoing and friendly rather than shy and retiring; administrators can be introvert, but they do need to be structured in their approach; journalists need to be flexible and confident. A person who is suited to one role might be hopeless in another. Understanding people and matching them to roles is where personality questionnaires and profiles can be so useful.

1 Why do employers measure personality?

Personality and work performance

Employers are looking for people who will work well in a job and have the skills and knowledge necessary to do their work to a high standard. Having the right skills doesn't always make the best employee, however. It is not only being *able* to do the job that is important, employers are also concerned about how the person approaches work and how well they fit into the organization. Some people approach work in a structured fashion, whereas others tend to develop better relationships with other members of staff, customers or suppliers. Some people like to do things in the same way all the time, and others like variety and will change the way they do things as often as they can. Depending on the job and the organization, these different approaches may be more or less suitable.

People have different levels of motivation for work and different things satisfy them. Some people work only for the pay and have little interest in the job itself. Obviously, some jobs are intrinsically more interesting than others, but some people are more likely than others to gain satisfaction from a task, no matter what it is. They gain satisfaction from a job well done, whether it is a happy customer, a problem solved, a project delivered on time or a clean floor. People can find motivation in interacting with others, working in a team, helping someone else, solving a problem, working out how something functions, wielding power and responsibility, being active and in many other ways.

Different jobs and organizations have a different potential to satisfy these personal needs. Jason, who likes achievements, might prefer a job with difficult goals and targets to reach. Jacinta might find constant striving for targets annoying or anxiety provoking. She might prefer a role where the pace of work was more measured and predictable, where she felt confident that she could accomplish everything that was needed and not have to worry about whether she could achieve what was required. Jason might find a job in sales with targets to achieve each month satisfying but an administrative job keeping records rather boring. Jacinta might find the administrative job appropriate and hate working in the sales environment. The way each person felt about a role would affect how they performed. All things being equal, it is likely that each person would work best in the role that best suited their personal style. It is, therefore, in both the employer's and the job seeker's interest to place people in jobs that suit their motivation and personality.

Working in a job that does not suit your personality generally requires more energy than one that is more in line with how you naturally behave. As an example of this consider Joanna and Josh, two tourist guides. Joanna, who is generally extroverted, likes talking to people and being the centre of attention, is happier in her work as a guide than Josh, who is naturally rather shy and is slow to develop a relationship when meeting new people. Josh has lots of interesting information to impart, but he can be perceived as a little cold and detached by those listening. He makes an effort to seem bright and entertaining to others and to amuse the group with jokes and humorous stories, and this does make his performance more successful. However, it is an effort for him, and at the end of the day he feels quite exhausted with putting on this act. When he is tired he finds it more difficult to maintain the façade and therefore becomes even less successful. Joanna, the more extrovert person, finds being bubbly and amusing quite natural and comes over to the group as warmer and more interested in them – at least superficially. It costs her little effort to be lively – in fact, she usually finds it energizing and ends the day on a high. The group enjoy Joanna's more natural performance more than Josh's efforts. Thus the person whose behavioural style best suits the job performs better in the role and gets more satisfaction from doing it.

This is a win – win situation for the employer and employee. The person who is less suited to the role in terms of personality enjoys it less and produces a reduced level of performance, and this is a less good outcome for both the employer and the employee.

Personality style also affects the ease with which someone might learn the new behaviours required in a role. In sales or customer service roles staff need to learn how to interact with people, perhaps how to deal with a difficult customer, how to handle a complaint and how to close a sale. All of these require interacting with other people and influencing them to modify their behaviour or attitude – become less aggressive, less angry or agree the purchase. There are techniques that are helpful in these situations, and with training anyone can become better at handling them. However, a person who is naturally comfortable interacting and influencing others is likely to find it easier to pick up such techniques and use them effectively than someone who is less outgoing or more task focused than people focused. The person with a personality that suits the requirements of the role is likely to take more away from training of this kind than the person who finds these behaviours more alien.

The examples so far are based on jobs that require interaction with people, and they contrasted people who are more extrovert with those who are more introvert. However, similar examples can be found that reflect other personality characteristics. For instance, some people are more rigid in their approach, preferring to do things according to the rules and to work in a consistent manner, whereas others are quite flexible, like to try different approaches, tend to ignore rules and do things as the feeling takes them. The former are better suited to roles where it is important to follow rules and structures – where there are health and safety procedures that must be followed, for example. They are likely to learn procedures more easily and will naturally follow them once they know them. On the other hand, they will feel uncomfortable in less structured jobs where there are no set procedures and everyone finds their own way of doing things or where they are dealing with constant change. The more flexible people will feel comfortable in this type of role but are likely to feel constrained when they are working in a more rule-bound environment. They are more likely to break rules or skip some stages in a task, and this could lead to errors or even serious accidents. Studies have shown that people with some personality characteristics are more likely to have driving and work-related accidents. When health and safety officers investigate accidents they frequently find that lack of concern for procedures is in large measure to blame. Even where there are other contributing factors, such as faulty materials or equipment, the accident could often have been avoided had proper procedures been followed. For instance, a recent marine accident investigation found two crew members on a fishing boat were hurt when they fell over 4 metres from lifting gear, which they had used to get them out of the hold. Using the lifting gear was quicker and required less effort, but was much more risky than climbing the portable ladder that was the safe (and prescribed) way of exiting the hold. People who are adventurous and risk taking in their personality are much more likely to take this kind of dangerous short cut than those who are cautious and follow rules.

The impact of situations on behaviour

Personality is not the only determinant of behaviour. Extroverts are more lively and talkative, and introverts tend to be quieter and more reflective. While some people are more extrovert than others, we all behave in a more extrovert manner in some situations than in others. When they are with close friends or family, people are more likely to be lively and talkative and share amusing stories; at work we may behave in a more formal manner, and at a job interview a person may talk only to answer questions. If you were to observe a teacher giving a lesson to a (well-behaved) class, it might seem that the teacher was the extrovert – doing all the talking, moving around the room, initiating interactions with the students. The students would seem like introverts sitting quietly listening, speaking only when asked.

However, the initial impression is likely to be false. Both the teacher's and the students' behaviour are determined largely by the situation – that is, how it is appropriate to behave in class if you are a teacher and if you are a student. It is not possible to determine from this type of observation the personalities of the students or the teacher. If we were to examine the people's behaviour more closely we might gain some more clues, but these also could be misleading. An extrovert teacher might tend to focus more on the individuals being taught, whereas an introvert might be more detached and less connected with the individual class members. But an experienced introvert teacher might have learned that it is important to maintain a connection with the class and make an effort to do so. Extrovert class members may find it more difficult to sit still and listen, and their discomfort with their role might be evident through fidgeting or other signs of restlessness. They may be quicker to respond to the teacher's questions and more likely to take opportunities to interact with others or contribute and speak up when doing so. On the other hand, an introvert student might be bored with the topic and also restless or have a high need to please others and therefore be willing to contribute when called on to do so.

If we consider the way we behave, particularly at work, far more of what we do is determined by the situation – the demands of the job or the expectations of our supervisor, colleagues or customers – than by anything to do with our own personality. When we speak and when we are silent, whether we sit still or move around, how much we help others, what we spend time thinking about, even how we dress and how we speak – these are all constrained by the requirements of the work we do and the organization we work for.

Job fit

If situations were the only determinant of our behaviour personality would not be a very important factor in the way people perform jobs. However, this is not the case. After the basic ability and skills of the job – word processing, cooking, dentistry, for example – research suggests that personality is the next most important indicator of suitability for a job. This is because although we can all moderate our behaviour to fit the needs of a situation, it can be hard to maintain the change over an extended period. The 'true' personality tends to come out, particularly in times of difficulty, fatigue or stress. The waiter who has been pleasant and attentive becomes taciturn and apathetic as the shift progresses; the computer programmer starts to lose concentration and make coding errors when a deadline is approaching.

Someone whose personality suits the role can behave naturally, but the person whose personality does not match the requirements of a role has to act a part, and this takes energy. Some roles require taking calculated risks. For instance, a buyer for a department store has to make the decision in summer about what quantity of winter coats to order for the next season, but the number sold will depend on how cold the winter will be and when the cold weather arrives. Order too few, and the store will miss out on potential sales; order too many, and the store will be left with stock it cannot sell. A buyer who is risk averse will find this type of decision very stressful and may tend to err on the side of caution or spend too much time seeking more information and therefore postpone the decision, leading to increased costs or delayed delivery dates. Someone who is a moderate risk taker will probably deal with the situation more easily, and because they experience less anxiety about the decisions they will be able to focus on what is known about the situation (trends in previous years, the accuracy of long-term weather forecasts, the quality of the goods on offer and so on) and not be distracted by worrying about things that cannot be known. Of course, an extreme risk taker might not make good decisions by tending to underestimate the potential downside of decisions. So, while anyone with the appropriate knowledge and experience could make the necessary decisions, someone with the most appropriate personality characteristics would be more likely to make a good decision and would feel comfortable with the need to make decisions when, of necessity, many of the facts are unknown.

Overall, the appropriate skills, knowledge and experience and/or the ability to learn them will be most important when selecting people for jobs, but after this the person's personality will be the next most important thing for ensuring a superior level of performance.

Organization fit

Personality can be important in judging if a person will be successful in doing a job, but it can also be relevant to determining how well a person will fit into a particular organization. Every company or organization has its own culture, its own way of doing things. Some organizations are very friendly, egalitarian and informal. Others may be more structured and hierarchical. In some companies people are expected to spend time helping other employees with their work, while in others people are expected to get on with their own jobs. Some companies monitor quite closely how people work, but others let employees get on with things as long as the outputs are all right. The quality of the product produced may be of paramount concern to one organization; another may pay more attention to the quantity produced. As you read this, you may already have sensed that you would feel more comfortable working in certain of these organizational cultures rather than others. Personality is a large factor in this kind of fit. Someone who is flexible and has a high tolerance of ambiguity will fit in better in Company A, which is unstructured and deals in a spontaneous manner with issues as they arise. The same person might find Company B, which has a very planned and controlled approach with lots of procedures that must be carefully followed and documented, stifling and bureaucratic. Someone who is more regulated and prefers a more predictable environment might be very happy with Company B but find Company A chaotic and disorganized.

What are questionnaires used for?

Personality questionnaires are used for a number of different purposes. One of the most frequent is in making recruitment, selection and promotion decisions. The information about candidates' personality style and how they approach things, relate to people, express their feelings and so on is relevant to how well they will perform in the job and fit into the organization. Personality profiles help in understanding how candidates might approach the job and the strengths and weaknesses associated with their approach.

Questionnaires and other tests are an efficient way of providing a lot of information about candidates. One administrator can administer a questionnaire to a number of candidates at the same time. Questionnaires can also be administered via a computer and over the internet, and computer-based report generation helps make the use of questionnaires very efficient. Interviews and other selection procedures tend to take up a lot of time, often of senior people. Questionnaires are objective and standardized measures, and they provide an additional perspective to that gained through other selection means.

Questionnaires are also used in development contexts. On an individual basis they can be used to help people better understand their personal style and how this might affect their performance. Insight into your personality is important in improving performance, and understanding how you naturally react to situations and people is a first step to developing more effective responses. For instance, being aware that you are the sort of person who dislikes change may help you check an immediate negative response to suggestions from others and consider them more on their merits. Being aware of how you seem to other people is also useful in adapting and developing your work style. All this can be gained through the use of personality questionnaires. Leadership development work often focuses on how people respond to others, and the use of questionnaires can facilitate this. Coaches use questionnaires with their clients to understand them better and to develop an appropriate plan of action with them.

Team building has the aim of helping groups of people to work better together. Questionnaires can help team members understand themselves and other team members better, and this can facilitate working together. When you understand why people respond as they do, it is often easier to be patient with them rather than becoming exasperated. For instance, realizing that Jose, one of the team members, likes to focus on one thing at a time will encourage you not to interrupt him unless necessary and to be less upset if he is a little impatient with you if you do interrupt him. Equally, being aware of how you come across to others may help you moderate your behaviour. For example, understanding that you are more of a risk taker than other people in the team will help you understand that their negative response to your suggestions is not personal but stems from their aversion to a more hazardous approach. You may need to set out your ideas more clearly and explain how you think the risks can be managed.

Personality questionnaires can also be useful when an employee is not performing well in a role, experiences conflict with colleagues or has other types of problems at work. The results from a questionnaires can provide insight into the individual's behaviour, the causes of friction or a difficulty with the job itself. This understanding can be used to help improve the individual's performance. It can sometimes identify and help the person understand a fundamental lack of fit with the role or organization and in this case may encourage a search for more suitable employment.

Career counsellors and outplacement consultants use questionnaires to understand people's behavioural style, interests and motivation. This helps them to suggest new and adapted career tracks for clients that are likely to suit their needs but that might not have been thought of otherwise. Young people finishing their education can benefit from this help, but it can also be useful for people who are looking for a change of career in later life, perhaps after having been made redundant or giving up a job through ill health or disability. Questionnaires can also help people understand the impression they make on others at selection interviews and develop better strategies for 'selling' themselves to new employers. In Chapter 4 there is some discussion of how different personality styles might affect how people go about searching and applying for jobs and how they approach different types of assessment.

2 What is personality?

Personality is a word used in everyday language, and in one sense it is well understood. However, the sense in which psychologists use the word is a little specialized. In everyday language we talk about people who have 'lots of personality' or who are 'lacking in personality'. For psychologists everyone has personality, but the word refers specifically to people's typical behavioural and emotional characteristics. It is what makes people into distinct individuals with their own patterns of thinking, feeling, responding to others and doing things. Someone described in everyday language as 'having personality' might actually be someone who is lively, animated and vivacious. Someone who is described as 'lacking personality' might be someone who is reserved, modest and quiet. For psychologists personality refers to people's preferences in a range of areas, including how they relate to others, their thinking and action style and their typical feelings and emotions.

The ancient Greeks referred to 'temperament' and differentiated four humours – sanguine, phlegm, choler and melancholy – which Shakespeare also used to describe his characters. Chinese philosophy uses the five elements – metal, water, wood, fire and earth – to classify many things, including people's temperament. Star signs are also associated with personality factors: Aries are said to be energetic and restless, Pisces are considered to be shy.

Although the nature of man has been discussed in philosophy and literature through the ages, it was the late nineteenth century before psychology was born as a science and personality began to be studied more carefully. Early theorists suggested that personality might be related to physical characteristics – for example, that stout people were outgoing in nature. One theory, phrenology, was based on relating irreg-ularities in the skull to personality factors. The work of people like Sigmund Freud and Carl Jung was influential in changing the way that personality was perceived. Their theories were particularly concerned with how personality might develop out of early childhood experiences.

The formal measurement of personality is mostly an invention of the twentieth century. In 1936 US psychologists Gordon Allport and H.S. Odbert collected over 18,000 English language adjectives that could describe people and researched them to determine how they might be categorized and systematized. This work has been central to the development of modern personality theory. They recognized that some words referred to physical characteristics – tall and plump, for example – and some referred to very temporary states – excited and surprised. The words most relevant to personality were those that referred to more enduring or stable characteristics that were not physical, such as bold and friendly.

We concentrate on characteristics that are stable and enduring because these will characterize people and are therefore relevant in thinking about people's behaviour over a long period – years rather than hours or days. We all have transitory moods – everyone experiences anger, sadness or exhilaration from time to time, for example – and these moods are typically a response to what is happening around us. This is not what we mean by personality. However, someone who has a tendency to anger easily might be described as fiery, excitable or irritable. These descriptions reflect a more stable characteristic or disposition, which can be thought of as part of the person's personality.

Although personality is made up of stable characteristics, this is not to say that personality cannot change over time. Our experiences throughout our lives, particularly in childhood, influence the way we see the world and how we respond to it. Such changes could be thought of as changes to our personality, but they are just as likely to be due to our better knowledge of ourselves. We develop ways of responding that suit us and our personality. Research suggests that personality is relatively stable over time. Old people who are extroverts were almost certainly extrovert as children. However, experience can modify some aspects of personality, and particularly traumatic experiences can have a major effect. Counselling and therapy can also effect change in some aspects of personality.

There is strong evidence for a genetic component in personality. This means that some of our personality traits are inherited from our parents and grandparents. Identical twins are found to be more similar in personality than fraternal twins, and twins who are reared apart – that is, adopted by different families at birth – are often found to share personality characteristics later in life. New parents become aware of the personality of their baby even in its first few months of life. This does suggest that some aspects of personality may be 'hard wired' into our make-up, and it might explain why personality tends to be relatively stable over time. Because personality tends to be stable, it makes sense to take it into account when looking at the suitability of people for jobs and developing their performance at work.

Although personality is relatively unchanging, behaviour can change. Introverts can learn to be socially skilled and to interact with others. They can become effective at typically non-introvert activities such as making presentations and leading a team. Equally extroverts can learn to behave in a quiet, restrained manner, and they may learn to appreciate more internally focused experiences, such as meditating. This does not mean that extroverts have become introverts, or vice versa. Rather, each has developed a broader perspective than that which comes naturally to them and has expanded their behavioural repertoire.

Psychologists sometimes invent new words to describe specific aspects of personality – for instance, it was Freud who invented the terms extrovert and introvert. However, for the most part, ordinary words are used to describe personality, although psychologists may be more exact about what they mean by a term than when it is used in everyday speech. Many adjectives can be thought of as personality descriptors – optimistic, cantankerous, cautious, ambitious and so on. The four humours discussed above can be thought of as personality traits. The choleric person is irritable; a phlegmatic individual tends to be lethargic; the melancholic person is brooding and morose; and a sanguine person is cheerful and optimistic.

Behavioural style

Behavioural style refers to personality characteristics that relate to how people act or respond to their environment – how they interact with other people, how they approach tasks and difficulties, how they feel and respond emotionally to things. Thus the same event or situation can be perceived positively and as attractive by one person and negatively by another. For instance, someone who is highly extrovert may be pleased to be invited to a party, look forward to the event with pleasure, behave in a lively and engaged manner at the party and afterwards feel energized by the event. Someone who is highly introverted may look forward with trepidation to a party and perhaps try to find excuses not to attend. At the party the introvert may be diffident, sitting on the sidelines and speaking to just a few very familiar people. Attending the event may be quite stressful and leave the person feeling tired and jaded with the effort of being sociable. This illustrates how personality can affect how events are perceived, how people think and feel about them and how they most naturally behave in response to those events.

Although it is difficult to control the way we perceive the world or what we think about it, we can control our behaviour. If we hear an upsetting remark or some criticism we think is unfair we can feel angry or humiliated, and we could give vent to these feelings by answering back in an angry manner or by running away. However, we do not have to act out these feelings. We can hide the degree to which the remarks affected us and offer a gentler denial or ignore the remark. It takes an effort of will to smother our feelings, but we all control our behaviour to some extent according to what we think is right or appropriate or because of the way we would like others to perceive us. It is harder to change the way we feel about the remark, to learn to take criticism as a positive learning opportunity and not to be hurt by it or become defensive. It is even harder to change the way we perceive the world, to stop seeing the remark as a criticism and to understand it as something else – the other person's attempt to help us improve or even the result of their own need for attention rather than any real response to our performance. However, all these elements are potentially subject to our own conscious control to some degree, if we have the desire and the energy to control our more natural response.

When we describe someone's personality we are thinking about their natural response rather than how they might have learned to respond. However, if learned responses become so well embedded that they become second nature then we can think of them as part of the personality. For most people, these learned responses are a thinner veneer, which can be maintained only with some investment of energy.

When employers measure personality they are particularly interested in how people behave in work situations. However, people do not change their personalities at work. Although they may moderate their behaviour in line with work requirements and conventions, they still have the same types of thoughts, feelings and behavioural instincts.

Personality can be broken down into a number of domains – for instance, motivation, attitudes, values, interests, behavioural style and thinking style – and we will explore some of these areas in more detail in Chapter 4. First, however, we will consider two ways of thinking about personality. These are traits and types.

Traits

Personality is often described in terms of traits or characteristics. A personality trait is a disposition to behave or respond in a particular manner. The idea of a personality trait is that it is a dimension of personality along which people can differ. We might think of people as having a little or a lot of a particular trait. Often the two extremes of a trait reflect contrasting personalities. Examples might be extrovert and introvert or highly anxious and calm people. People at either extreme of the trait typically tend to have opposite reactions to the same situation. Extroverts, for example, have a positive response to meeting new people, whereas introverts might find this rather a trial. Introverts enjoy an evening engaging in a solitary pastime such as reading or craftwork; extroverts, on the other hand, would find this at best a dull way to spend so much time.

The trait can be thought of as a continuum, with some people distinctly at one end and some people distinctly at the other. Most people, however, will be somewhere between these two extremes. We could imagine taking a class full of people and lining them up with the most anxious at the extreme right of the line and the most relaxed at the extreme left. We could order the people in the line so that everyone was at least as anxious as everyone to their left and no more anxious than everyone to their right.

Figure 1: People lined up by their level of anxiety

Very relaxed   Moderately relaxed   Neither relaxed   Moderately anxious   Very anxious
nor anxious

In personality assessment we try to assign numerical scores that reflect where individuals fall on this line between the two extremes of a trait. A scale of a personality questionnaire is a set of questions that can be used to assign scores to an individual for a particular trait. It is typically found that there are many people with a moderate position on the line or scale and relatively few people with more extreme scores – that is, most of us are neither extremely relaxed nor extremely anxious. Rather, the majority are reasonably calm and alert rather than overly anxious or extremely relaxed. There is also a substantial proportion of people who are more anxious than this, but few who are very anxious and stressed most of the time. Similarly, there is a substantial proportion of people who are moderately relaxed most of the time, but few who are nearly always severe and relaxed.

In understanding individuals we look at their position on scales measuring a variety of personality traits. This is often referred to as a personality profile. For instance, Jay may be described as a very structured individual, who is moderately extroverted, is imaginative and likes change, is moderately helpful and sympathetic to others but can be quite anxious. Personality profiles are often provided in diagrammatic form. For instance, Jay's profile might look like this:

Figure 2: Personality profile for Jay

Unstructured			<>	Structured
Introvert		<>		Extrovert
Down to earth			<>	Imaginative
Independent		<>		Sympathetic
Anxious	<>			Relaxed

Of course, this description and the profile are an abbreviated description of the person. Jay is described as 'structured', and this may be the name of the scale used in the personality questionnaire, but 'structured' will have an exact meaning in this context that will have been defined by the questionnaire's developers, and it would not be possible to know exactly what it implied without being familiar with the questionnaire itself. It might, for example, include some or all of the following: planful, tidy, inflexible, disciplined, conscientious, rigid, neat, punctual, ordered, controlled and forward thinking.

The principle of a profile should be clear, however. It provides a picture of the individual in terms of the personality traits measured, and this can be interpreted by someone who is trained in the use of the personality questionnaire. From the profile an experienced tester can derive a portrait of the person's behavioural style and emotional responses, and this can be used in determining the person's suitability for a job. Of course, it can have many other uses, including helping a person to understand themselves better, advising individuals on their development needs or helping them to work better in a team or as a manager.

Traits can be quite broad, encompassing a wide range of behaviours, or narrow, relating to only a specific aspect of behavioural style. Extroversion is a broad trait as it refers both to the way a person feels and acts with other people and also to their mood (extroverts tend to be lively and cheerful). Extroversion can also encompass narrower traits such as emotional control, outspokenness, energy, optimism and (lack of) modesty. These traits are grouped together in the broad extroversion trait because they typically occur together. Someone who is outgoing is more likely to be energetic than lethargic. A trait such as emotional control is much narrower than extroversion, because it refers only to how a person controls the expression of their emotions to others. Extroverts tend to be lower on emotional control than introverts, but this is only one aspect of their behaviour.

Broad traits provide a description of personality at a very general level, whereas narrow traits are needed for more detailed descriptions. Broad traits allow for short, relatively simple descriptions of personality, which can provide a good overview without becoming bogged down in detail. However, they may be over generalized and not reflect the exact personality style of the individual. They may overlook ways in which a person is different from the norm of people with similar positions on a broad trait.

Narrow traits are more useful when a detailed description of a person's behavioural style is needed because they can be used to make fine discriminations. Someone who is generally highly extrovert may have more emotional control than is usual for people in this group, and narrower trait descriptions make it possible to elicit these fine distinctions. However, this will require a longer and more detailed description, which may be more than is required for some purposes. When working with narrower trait descriptions it is possible to lose sight of the overall personality of an individual through concentrating on the detail of specific aspects of their behaviour.

Questionnaires designed for a broad level of description typically have between four and eight scales. Questionnaires that have narrower scales tend to have 16 to 30 scales to cover all aspects of personality, and they typically take longer to complete. When employers are deciding which personality questionnaire to use, they will try to choose one that will provide an appropriate level of description of the individual for the purpose in question, but when a broad level of description is appropriate it must be remembered that this can conceal some fine distinctions. Measuring at a fine level will require a longer questionnaire. Some broad traits are described in Chapter 4, along with some of the narrower traits that could be embedded within them.

Types

Some personality theorists disagree with a trait-based approach. One criticism of the approach is that it is purely descriptive – that is, it tells us *how* people behave or think but not *why* they do what they do. It cannot explain why some people develop in one way and others in another. Type theories of personality are also generally used in a descriptive manner, but they are often supported by an underlying theory of how types emerge and develop.

In the discussion of traits above we looked at the four humours as personality traits. However, it might be better to characterize these as personality types. Although we could imagine a person who is both irritable and lethargic, the humours were actually conceived as personality types. People were not thought of as being moderately melancholic and moderately sanguine, very choleric but not at all phlegmatic. Rather, each person was thought to be of one particular humour. The rather strange names are because the humours were thought to be caused by excesses in different bodily fluids – for example, the sanguine personality was fed by the blood. The star signs are also types in that your birthdate determines the zodiac category you belong to. Even if you are born close to the cusp between two star signs it is the controlling sign at the time of birth that is most important. You are not a mixture of the two.

One type theory of personality that is the basis for a commonly used personality questionnaire, the Myers–Briggs Type Indicator(®), is founded on the work of Carl Jung. He initially worked closely with

Freud but over time developed his own theory of personality. He suggested that there are different modes of interacting with the world, and when we are quite young we develop preferences for certain of these modes. Because of these preferences we develop some modes more than others, and these become our typical behavioural style. For instance, we can focus on the here and now of what we see, hear and sense in other ways to gain a practical acquaintance with the world, or we can perceive things more indirectly through our understanding of what they are or their possibilities and potential. One person, for example, might experience a garden in terms of the colours and scents of the flowers, the sound of bird song and the feel of walking on grass. For another person the same garden might trigger a raft of thoughts – about the ecosystem as a whole, the signs of the impact of pollution or how symbolic it is of the interconnectedness of all living things. These two modes of perception, one with a practical focus on perception and the other with a more abstract focus on intuitions and possibilities, are not on a continuum: they are fundamentally different ways of approaching things.

Having developed a preference for one of these modes we will tend to use it more than the other. We will, therefore, become more skilled and used to using that approach, and we will be more comfortable using that way of perceiving the world. It will become natural to us to adopt that approach rather than the other, and it will become our dominant way of perceiving things. We will still be able to use the alternate mode, but it will be less well developed, more awkward and less familiar to us. We will most naturally use our chosen way. Thus the theory explains how types develop as they do.

Because these alternate modes are fundamentally different, people belong to either one or the other. Further, the theory says that once you have chosen a preference for a particular mode you develop the behaviour and thinking style that are typical of that mode even further. If we were to characterize a class full of people by type they would be in separate silos, each belong to one group or the other.

Figure 3: People arranged by type

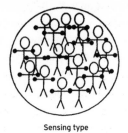
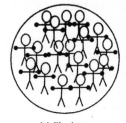

Sensing type   Intuitive type

In the questionnaire based on Jung's theory a person's type is determined not just by the mode of perceiving (see above) but by three other areas or personality dimensions, each of which has two alternate modes. One of these dimensions is extroversion and introversion. This dimension can be thought of as a continuum, as discussed in the section on traits. However, Jung's view was that extroverts and introverts represent fundamentally different types. Extroverts are focused on the outside world of other people and things, whereas introverts are directed by their own inner world of thoughts and feelings. Introverts evaluate things internally before trying them out in public. They think things through before acting. They are more socially self-sufficient than extroverts, who need to try out ideas on other people to see how they will react. Extroverts need to use the outside world as a sounding board in order to understand their own behaviour and feelings. Extroverts often feel that they need to talk through an idea with someone in order to evaluate it. This leads to a strong need to be with other people, and extroverts have a more active experimental approach to doing things than introverts. Introverts tend to think things through internally before engaging in any action. Again, these are fundamentally different ways of approaching things, and Jung's theory says that once we have a slight preference for one over the other, it will tend to develop more so that we become much more effective and more comfortable at using that approach than the other, and it will colour our way of interacting with the world.

We have now discussed two of the dimensions of the Myers–Briggs Type Indicator: sensing–intuiting and extrovert–introvert. The other two are: thinking–feeling and perceiving–judging. As with the sensing–intuiting and extrovert–introvert dimensions, these also have specific meanings within the theory rather than what might be expected from everyday language. A person's personality type is revealed by evaluating which four choices they make. There are 16 possible personality types, and these are determined by four choices between two modes. One of the most common personality types is the extrovert–sensing–thinking–judging type (ESTJ). These people tend to be realistic and practical and good at organizing and managing. They take a rational rather than an intellectual approach, come to decisions quickly but may sometimes ride rough shod over other people's feelings. A different type is the introvert–sensing–feeling–perceiving type (ISFP). They have one element in common with ESTJs, but are very different in style. ISFPs are quiet, friendly and loyal. Modest about themselves, they dislike disagreements. You may need to get to know an ISFP well to appreciate their warmth and flexibility. Each of the other 14 types can be similarly characterized.

One of the advantages of a type approach to personality is that it is possible to combine the different facets of personality into an integrated understanding of the whole person in terms of their particular type. The individual's overall personality type, which may stem from a combination of a number of type dimensions, is seen as a united whole rather than as a series of independent features. Most people find their type descriptions quite accurate and insightful. One of the difficulties with type theories is that the approach is about sorting people into categories, and some people may not fit any of the posited categories very well. It is not possible to take an intermediate position on any of the dimensions. For instance, types based on Jungian theory do not allow you to be both analytic (thinking) and warm (feeling).

3 Measuring personality

While the science of measuring personality is relatively young, people have been assessing personality for a long time. The Book of Judges in the Bible describes how Gideon chooses his fighting men for a battle (7:6). He watches all the soldiers drink from a spring after a long march and chooses only those who remain alert and ready to fight while drinking, rejecting those who put down their swords and shields and bend down to the water to drink. He was selecting those who were fully focused on their duty as soldiers over those who were sidetracked by their personal needs, in this case thirst.

Whenever we meet people we do in some sense assess their personality. When we are introduced to someone we will quite quickly make some judgements about whether they seem friendly and warm or cold and distant, whether they are quiet and reserved or lively and outspoken. These are all personality factors. However, we are not always very accurate in making these judgements. Research suggests that we make judgements about another person within only a few seconds of meeting them and that we are quite resistant to changing these judgements, even if the person's later behaviour does not exactly match our initial evaluation. One study found that people can make these judgements within milliseconds of seeing a picture of someone yet have no possibility of understanding their personality or behaviour from this exposure.

Deciding on what sort of personality an employer might be looking for and how this is determined is discussed in Chapter 5. Here we are concerned with how personality can be assessed.

Selection interviews

The most common way of evaluating job candidates is through the selection interview. This is used almost universally by employers to check out a candidate's suitability for a job. Although interviews are versatile selection tools that can provide information on many different facets of a person's suitability, research suggests that they are not always effective and are neither the most efficient nor most accurate way of measuring someone's personality. An interview allows the employer and the candidate to interact and evaluate each other. It allows the interviewer to ask about any relevant topic – the candidate's education and experience, previous employers, ambition and motivation and expectations of the workplace. Many employers will also say that they want to evaluate the 'fit' of the candidate to the job and the organization through the interview. This often means that they are trying to assess something about the person's personality and whether it is suitable. The interviewer wants to know if this is the sort of person who would work well within the organization, get on with other people and respond well to the way things are done in the organization.

There are, however, some problems, both general and specific, about using an interview to assess a person's personality. Research suggests that the interview is not always an effective way of collecting information about candidates. Unstructured interviews in particular are poor at differentiating promising from unlikely candidates. One reason for this could be the skill of the interviewer. Many interviewers are affected by our tendency to make quick evaluative judgements about people (see above). It has been found that typically interviewers decide quickly whether they think that the person they are interviewing is a likely candidate. If they think the person has potential they tend to concentrate on collecting evidence to support this view. They might, for example, ask the candidate to tell them about a successful project. On the other hand, if their initial judgement is that the candidate is poor they will look for evidence to confirm this view. They might for example, ask the candidate to tell them about a project that went wrong.

This seeking for evidence that confirms preconceived ideas is a typical strategy for evaluating information. Used alone, however, it is quite a poor strategy. People have to be trained to look for evidence that might contradict their initial impression to avoid making mistakes. Interviewers look for failings in people they expect to fail and successes in people they expect to succeed but not always vice versa. They need to be trained to look for success and failings in all candidates.

Structured interviews by trained interviewers are much better tools for identifying effective workers. However, even here there can be problems. Not all candidates are able to express themselves well at interview. Some people find it difficult to put into words their past experience and suitability for a role, whereas others are willing to sing their own praises and give a positive image at interview. Some people are more modest and underrate their skills and suitability. Some people become anxious at interview or when they are meeting new people, and this can affect the impression they make even when social skills are not required in the role. If you are the sort of person who finds it difficult to 'sell' yourself at interview you will appreciate the problem.

If the interview is the only method used to evaluate candidates, those who are poor communicators will lose out, even if good communication is not an important factor in the job. Using a number of different methods of assessing candidates means that the employer can get a more rounded picture of the candidate, which will not be biased by how well a candidate performs in a particular type of exercise. Using personality questionnaires, written exercises or role plays are all ways of extending the selection process to look at candidates in different ways and gain more information about them.

A further problem with interviews is that they can be quite subjective. An interviewer may have a personal response to something the candidate says. For instance, an interviewer may dislike a particular turn of phrase and make a negative evaluation of a candidate who uses it a great deal in speech or dislike a candidate because they have a hobby to which the interviewer has an aversion. It is quite difficult not to be swayed by your own personal likes and dislikes in evaluating another person.

Finally, assessing personality at interview can be particularly difficult. It requires great skill as an interviewer and a deep understanding of personality and how it affects behaviour. In particular, as the interviewee is trying to make a positive impression, they are probably not behaving in a typical manner. For instance anxiety and tension can affect how the person comes across.

Psychological measures of personality

There are many different ways of measuring personality. Some personality measures were developed for use in clinical and educational psychology. Many people have heard of the Rorschach inkblot test, which is a measure of personality and which belongs to the category of projective tests. The person being assessed is shown an inkblot and asked to say what it looks like. The task is vague, and the person being assessed projects their own ideas of what type of response to make. Another projective method of assessment is the sentence completion, in which the person being assessed is provided with the beginnings of sentences and asked to complete them. For instance:

When I think of my mother I . . .
I am most happy when I . . .

Projective tools are primarily designed for use in understanding psychological problems and pathology, and highly trained psychologists are required to interpret the results. They are not intended for use in selecting people for work or in other occupational contexts. The types of questionnaire used by employers that you might meet when applying for a job tend to be much more straightforward and focus on typical personality characteristics, not abnormal ones.

Personality questionnaires

You might have come across psychological questionnaires in newspapers and magazines. These are usually not professionally developed questionnaires, but rather a selection of questions put together to illustrate a particular issue. The questions are often poorly written, and it is not unusual to find that none of the responses really describes how you would behave. These are not the kind of questions that are put in properly developed questionnaires that are designed for use in staff selection and development.

Example of a magazine type quiz: 'Are you a good "best friend"?'

1. How often do you call your best friend?
    a. Once in a while
    b. Everyday
    c. Every hour
    d. Never, my friend calls me

2. On meeting your best friend after a long time apart what do you say?
    a. Let me tell you what has happened to me!
    b. Tell me all about what you have been up to
    c. Why haven't you been in touch?
    d. You don't say anything special, it's as if you hadn't been apart

3. Your best friend does not like you new boyfriend/girlfriend. What do you do?
    a. Find a new best friend
    b. Trust your best friend's judgement and drop the new boyfriend/girlfriend.
    c. Try to find time to see your best friend separately.
    d. Expect your best friend to put up with your new boyfriend/girlfriend as a loyal best friend.

4. You have just got back from work after a late shift, you are
   hungry and tired and you still have a pile of preparation to do
   for tomorrow. Your best friend rings in tears. Do you
   a. Arrange to see your friend later in the week when you are
      not so busy and tired and can be more help
   b. Drop everything and rush round to be with your friend
   c. Talk to your friend on the phone while you get something
      to eat
   d. Tell your friend you will ring back later when you have
      done your work

There are various names for personality questionnaires. Some people
refer to them as tests, but this is not accurate because the word implies
something that can be passed or failed. The word 'test' is usually
reserved for assessments of 'maximal performance' – that is, where a
skill, knowledge or ability is being measured and the focus is to find
out how well a person can perform. Most school tests are assessments
of maximal performance, as are psychometric ability tests commonly
used in staff selection – verbal or numerical reasoning tests, for example. You may be asked to complete ability tests together with, or
instead of, a personality questionnaire when you are applying for a
job. The word 'inventory' is often used instead of questionnaire, and it
suggests going through all the elements of a person's personality and
listing them. Inventory can be used interchangeably with questionnaire. Sometimes a questionnaire is called a 'survey'. This can be
misleading, because it suggests market research rather than personality assessment. Personality questionnaires can also be referred to as
'personality measures' or 'personality instruments'. These different
titles do not have any specific implications for the content of the questionnaire.

The proper development of a personality questionnaire requires
the involvement of a team of psychologists, including experts in

questionnaire design, in personality theory and in psychometric statistics. It is a process that takes, at the least, many months and often a number of years. The project includes conceptual phases, when the ideas of what is to be measured and how to measure it are developed, writing and reviewing phases, when the questions are created, trialling phases, when the embryo questionnaire is completed by hundreds of people, and statistical analysis phases, when the results of trials are reviewed to check whether the results meet the appropriate psychometric benchmarks. If necessary, the questionnaire is revised in the light of the results and retrialled. There are rarely fewer than two revisions, and often many more. In addition to this basic process of questionnaire development, research is performed to understand in more detail how well the questionnaire works and how to use it most effectively.

The result of this is that well-developed questionnaires encapsulate a great deal of knowledge and expertise in personality assessment and make this accessible to a much less expert user. They are sophisticated tools that enable a relatively unskilled person to assess personality effectively and accurately. While questionnaires are sophisticated tools, most questionnaires are essentially straightforward. They provide job candidates, or others completing them, with a way of describing their personality that is simple and easy to understand. The detailed development work is to create an instrument that is clear and unambiguous.

The last stage of development is the creation of a comparison group to use in interpreting the questionnaire results. Most questionnaires are interpreted by comparing an individual's results with that of a large relevant population, such as working adults or managers and professionals. Rather than looking at people's absolute score on a scale, their relative position is considered. This helps to put the score in context and enables more accurate differentiations between different scores on a scale. A typical scale score will be assigned to between 5 and 10 score categories or bands for the purpose of interpretation.

The information that questionnaires provide is typically straightforward. The purpose is to elicit from the people completing the questionnaire the knowledge they already have about their personality. However, the questionnaire helps to structure the knowledge and provide a metric, or a scale, in which to understand it. If you know yourself well, the results of the questionnaire will probably tell you what you already know. What it will do is put this information into a structure that may allow you to make better use of it. It will also help another person to understand you. Questionnaires used in staff selection will restrict themselves to appropriate aspects of personality. You will not be revealing information about yourself that a normal person would not be happy to reveal in other job selection contexts such as an interview or application form.

Advantages of the questionnaire approach

All psychometric tests and questionnaires have a number of attributes that make them effective measures of people's qualities. They are standardized tasks to which people can respond on the basis of their own skills, abilities and characteristics. Each person receives the same questions or tasks and is given exactly the same instructions. All responses are scored in the same way to provide the personality profile or type. This standardization allows us to infer that the differences in the way that different people respond are due to differences between them rather than the task itself or particular circumstances. This is not true of much other information collected during the selection process, when the interviewer might phrase questions differently for different candidates, or the 'chemistry' between the interviewer and the interviewee will differ, which can affect the way questions are asked and how the candidate responds.

Questionnaires are developed by experts who understand what it is they are trying to measure and how to measure it. They structure information about personality so that it is easier to understand. Rather than a series of stories or disconnected facts, personality questionnaires provide structured information within a profile that can be meaningfully interpreted.

Questionnaires also provide objective information about the

individual. Because their administration and scoring are standardized there is no place for the opinions or biases of any individual to affect the results. While most employers attempt to make their selection processes as objective as possible, the reality is that every assessor or interviewer has their own personal prejudices and preconceived notions about people. They may, consciously or unconsciously, find a particular accent suggestive of competence or incompetence, or they may discount some experiences and overvalue others – for example, they may not realize the experience that can be acquired in helping in the home but overestimate what can be gained from participating in team sports – or they may be more likely to believe someone who is attractive over someone who is plainer in looks. A common finding of people who have unclear speech because of a disability is that other people underestimate their intelligence. This type of subjective attitude can lead to errors in assessing people, but objective questionnaires help to counter this subjectivity.

Research shows that well-developed questionnaires can be effective tools in selecting people for jobs. The use of questionnaires can help in the appointment of people who are likely to be more successful in jobs, who fit in better to organizations, who are less likely to fail in the job, who are easier to train and who are less likely to leave after only a short period of service. This makes them very useful for employers. It is also in candidates' interests to be selected for a job in which they are likely to succeed. Candidates are likely to be happier and more satisfied in their roles, and being successful in a role is, in itself, a benefit. We would all rather succeed than fail.

Questionnaires are developed to provide a high degree of consistency – that is, if you take a questionnaire twice, your results should be very similar. If two people who are similar in personality both complete a questionnaire they should each receive similar results. Typically, questionnaires are more consistent or reliable than other types of assessment. Different interviewers can come to different opinions about the same candidate, and candidates may perform better in one interview than in another. This can be because they get on better with one interviewer than another or because their ideas flowed better on one occasion than another. The standardization of questionnaires is helpful in maintaining a high level of consistency, but the detailed development process, during which the degree of reliability is carefully measured and monitored, ensures that precision of measurement is high.

Because of their standardization and objectivity, questionnaires are also likely to be fairer than many other selection processes. Everyone receives the same task in the same way. There are no helpful hints for one candidate that others do not also get. In addition, during the development process a great deal of attention is generally paid to ensuring that the content of a questionnaire is appropriate for all types of respondents. This was not always the case, however, and in the past some questionnaires included material that was inappropriate or unsuitable for certain groups. Questionnaires designed for selecting managers might have assumed, for example, that the candidates would be male, and culture differences between groups were not taken into account. Modern questionnaire developers are much more sophisticated and aware of these issues and will take them into account in developing and researching questionnaires.

Questionnaire designs

The majority of questionnaires used in a work context are based on the individual choosing or responding to statements or words according to how well they describe them. Typically, you will be presented with a series of words or statements and asked to rate or rank them in some way. On the following pages are some examples of the kinds of questions you might be asked in a personality questionnaire. Such questionnaires are measures of 'typical performance' – that is, they are trying to assess how a person usually behaves, not the extremes of how they might behave in extraordinary circumstances. Other tests, either psychometric tests of ability, such as numerical and verbal reasoning tests, or school examination, are tests of 'maximal performance', which are designed to measure the best a person can possibly do in a field of performance.

Some questionnaires are very short, with only a single page of questions. However, questionnaires are often much longer and may have 200 or more questions. Longer questionnaires tend to provide more accurate and more detailed results, but they take some time to complete – up to an hour is not unusual. There is a trade-off between the length of the questionnaire and the detail of information about personality that can be gathered and the accuracy of measurement. Short questionnaires generally provide less detailed results but are quicker to complete. Some questionnaires look at as few as four or five aspects of personality, whereas others measure 30 or more. Employers will choose the design that best suits their needs, depending on how they want to use the results.

Some questionnaires are designed specifically for use in an employment context. These have questions or other content that are chosen to be relevant to the way people behave at work. Other questionnaires are designed for more general use, not only employment, and they tend to have broader content, which may include references to topics that are not relevant to work – relating to friends and hobbies, for example, not just employment and work contacts. A further group of questionnaires has been designed for clinical use with people who have psychological problems, and these can have very varied content and may sometimes even seem bizarre. They are not appropriate for use in a mainstream occupational context, and you should not be presented with them during a selection process. Only on rare occasions, such as when an employer refers an employee to a psychologist with some emotional problems, might such a questionnaire be used within employment.

Questionnaires can sometimes feel quite repetitive when you complete them. Some themes seem to be repeated throughout the questionnaire, and you may feel that you have already answered some of the questions. This is, in fact, unlikely, because questionnaires rarely repeat questions exactly. However, they frequently use a few quite similar questions to enhance the accuracy of measurement and the ability to differentiate between people. Repetition can also check the consistency of responses.

Because questionnaires are standardized instruments not all parts of every questionnaire will be relevant to every job. You may become aware of this when you are answering a questionnaire and some of the questions do not seem important for the sort of job you are applying for. Typically, an employer will look only at the relevant parts of the questionnaire in deciding on someone's suitability for the job.

There are several styles of content in questionnaires. Some ask you to rate or otherwise respond to single words – 'friendly' or 'focused' – and others use simple phrases and statements, such as 'Honesty is the best policy', 'I will say what I mean'. Some questionnaires use quite long and specific statements, such as 'When working on a project I need to understand what the main purpose of the work is to help me focus.' Much of the content of the type of questionnaire you will meet in an occupational context is quite transparent – that is, it is clear what is being asked and what its relevance is to work situations.

Some questionnaire developers feel that this approach encourages people to try to distort their answers. They prefer to use a more opaque style of question, which is difficult to relate directly to performance at work or common personality traits but which has been shown through research to relate to them. For instance, if it were known that introverts had a slight preference to write with a pencil whereas extroverts were more likely to prefer writing with a pen, you might include a question like 'Do you prefer to write with a pencil or a pen?' These relationships are usually quite weak, and many questions of this type are required to be sure of a person's personality. However, because this type of question can appear to be unrelated to any job or employment context, it is not possible to guess what they are measuring or what would be the desirable response. You will see that some of these more opaque questions are included in the examples below.

Example question styles

Some questionnaires ask you to rate statements in different ways. This may be just agree or disagree, true or false, or it may be according to different types of rating scales. Below are some examples of rating question types.

1. Say whether you agree or disagree with the following statements.

I like learning new facts.	Agree	Disagree
I generally feel confident in company.	Agree	Disagree
I rarely get emotional.	Agree	Disagree
It is better to try and fail than not to try at all.	Agree	Disagree
People cannot always be trusted.	Agree	Disagree
People like me because I am always willing to help them when they have problems.	Agree	Disagree
One of my favourite things is starting to write in a new notebook.	Agree	Disagree

2. Use the rating scale below to show how accurately each statement describes you.

1	2	3	4	5
Very inaccurate	Moderately inaccurate	Neither inaccurate nor accurate	Moderately accurate	Very accurate

RESPONSE

When I meet a new person I am usually the one to start a conversation.	
People describe me as friendly.	
I am the sort of person who nails my colours to the mast.	

RESPONSE

I generally do what I am told.	
It makes me uncomfortable to have to tell a lie.	
I enjoy being in charge of others and telling people what to do.	
I sometimes listen to the radio and watch television at the same time.	

3. Rate the extent to which you agree or disagree with each of the following statements using the following scale.

1	2	3	4
Strongly disagree	Disagree	Agree	Strongly agree

RESPONSE

It is important to me to achieve my targets.	
I like to do a good job.	
I sometimes get upset.	
I enjoy meeting new people.	
When I hear a word I don't know I like to find out its meaning.	
I set myself achievable targets, make plans to achieve them and set up milestones so I can tell how I am doing against the targets.	
I prefer listening to the radio than watching television.	

4. Ask yourself, how frequently do I engage in the behaviour described? The rating scale runs from one to eight; choose the number that best applies to each statement.

1	Almost never	5	Fairly often
2	Rarely	6	Usually
3	Once in a while	7	Very frequently
4	Sometimes	8	Almost always

RESPONSE

Not do something that I have promised to do.	
Tell other people honestly what I think of them.	
Go out of my way to help someone with their work.	
Let my hair down after a hard week.	
Set myself challenging goals to achieve.	
Do something I have never done before just to experience the novelty.	
Check what the weather will be the next day.	

Some questionnaires ask you to choose between different options. Sometimes the choices are two opposites – being alone, being with people, for instance – but sometimes the options are a selection of different things – being with people, doing something creative. Here you are being asked what your preference is. For some sets of options the choice may be quite clear for you. At other times you may find that you quite like all the options and sometimes you may not really agree with any of them. Even if you have only a minor preference for one thing over another, choose that. Across all the choices in the questionnaire your real personality should come through. Here are some examples for you to try.

5. Circle the answer that best describes you for each statement.

	A	B
When I am with other people I tend to be	Lively	Quiet
When I am working I would rather	Start a new place of work	Finish something I am doing
I would most like to work with	People	Animals
When I am upset I am most likely to	Find a friend to talk to	Think things through on my own
I prefer work that is	Stimulating	Organized
I am more likely to give feedback if someone has	Done something well	Made an error
I like to wear clothes that	Have a strong pattern	Are plain colours

6. Circle the answer that best describes you for each statement.

	A	B	C
I prefer to work	On my own	With another person	In a team
I like work that is	Familiar	In between	Novel
When things are changing I find it	Exciting	In between	Worrying

Circle the answer that best describes you for each statement.

	A	B	C
If someone is rude to me I am most likely to	Be angry	Ignore it	Feel hurt
If I give a presentation I like to	Prepare well in advance	In between	Talk spontaneously
When it is very important to me to achieve a goal I	Ask others for help	Just do my best	Work late
When I go out I am mostly likely to go to	A theatre or cinema	A restaurant	A club

7. Which statement in each pair is most like you?

A	B
I am easily bored.	I keep my work space tidy.
I am a good listener.	I like to beat the opposition.
I always meet deadlines.	I want to be surrounded by beautiful things.
I have a lot of creative ideas.	I think people should sort out their own problems.
I often take work worries home.	I play by the rules.
I look for innovative ways of improving my performance.	I persuade people by explaining my ideas clearly.
I always know how much money I have in my bank account.	I take time to get some fresh air every day.

8. For each set of four words choose the one that is most like you and
   the one that is least like you.

	MOST LIKE ME	LEAST LIKE ME
Lively		
Focused		
Caring		
Outspoken		

Trustworthy		
Imaginative		
Tidy		
Soft hearted		

Gentle		
Dependable		
Special		
Flexible		

Firm		
Energetic		
Emotional		
Curious		

Analytic		
Competitive		
Friendly		
Structured		

Garden		
Lighthouse		
Castle		
Library		

9. For each set of three statements choose the one that is most like you and the one that is least like you.

	MOST LIKE ME	LEAST LIKE ME
Choosing something from a menu I have never had before		
Doing things by the book		
Making new friends		

	MOST LIKE ME	LEAST LIKE ME
Lending an ear to someone's problems		
Worrying about the future		
Thinking up new ways of doing things		

	MOST LIKE ME	LEAST LIKE ME
Planning a project		
Telling a joke		
Saying what I think		

	MOST LIKE ME	LEAST LIKE ME
Analysing numerical data		
Looking for the flaws in a plan		
Focusing on achieving my targets		

	MOST LIKE ME	LEAST LIKE ME
Coordinating the team's activities		
Telling people what I think		
Asking other people for their opinion		

	MOST LIKE ME	LEAST LIKE ME
When I make an error I see it as a learning opportunity		
I think it is more important to tell people why we are doing something than how to do it		
When I make a promise I will keep it, even if it costs me a great deal of effort		

	MOST LIKE ME	LEAST LIKE ME
Sharing a sandwich with a friend		
Staying up all night		
Worrying about what to wear for work		

Other approaches to measuring personality

There are other approaches to measuring personality apart from question-naires and other psychological tools. The use of the interview to evaluate personality was discussed above and found generally wanting in the hands of most interviewers. However, as a candidate you should be aware that an interviewer may well be looking at your general demeanour and patterns of response to people and situations as well as evidence of your skills, expe-rience and competence that are relevant to the role. In addition to the interview, facets of personality may be assessed through other kinds of exercise. The rest of this chapter reviews the main types of assessment you may meet during recruitment, selection or development activities, which might be being used in part to understand your personality.

Role plays

Many employers use a variety of interactive exercises in assessment, including various kinds of role play, where the candidate must interact according to a given brief. In a development or promotion context these exercises allow participants to show how they might cope with scenarios outside their current responsibilities. The content is typically relevant to the job or employing organization, but not always. For external candidates for a job, role plays can be designed to provide an opportunity to display behaviours that would be relevant to the job but that do not require specific job or organizational information that someone from outside the organization may not have.

The assessment of the candidate is made by an observer who watches how the candidate goes about the task. Typically, a number of different areas of competence are evaluated. Some of these may relate to skills and abilities, but generally some will be related to personality factors. The competencies to be evaluated will depend on the requirements of the role for which the candidate is applying.

Examples of personality-related factors that might be evaluated include:

- Influencing – did the person influence others to his or her point of view?
- Leadership – did the person tend to take a lead in the discussion, coordinating how the group approached the task?
- Team working – did the person promote team working, encourage quiet group members to participate and allow others to speak?
- Organization – did the person approach the task in an organized manner, consider all the issues, use the time effectively and so on?
- Empathy – did the person show an understanding of the perspective and feelings of other people in the scenario?

Role plays may be one-on-one exercises in which the candidate speaks to an individual with a particular purpose. Examples of individual role play exercises include:

- The candidate plays the role of a customer services officer and talks to a customer who has a complaint. The candidate is required to find out the details of the complaint and resolve it, keeping within company policy but leaving the customer satisfied.

- The candidate is given the role of a sales executive who must introduce the product range to a new client and try to gain an initial order.
- The candidate plays the role of a supervisor who must give feedback to a member of staff who has several performance issues.
- The candidate plays the role of buyer who must try to negotiate a more advantageous contract with a key supplier.

Role plays can also involve more than one person. In a *group exercise* several candidates will be asked to perform a task together. Sometimes all the candidates are provided with the same brief, but sometimes each candidate is given a slightly different brief. In general, the task of the group is to discuss the matter in hand and reach some conclusions on how to deal with it or the next steps to take. In some group exercises one person is appointed the leader, but more often there is no designated leader. Group exercises might include:

- The group play the role of managers in an organization and are asked to make a recommendation on whether to accept a proposal to introduce a new product line to a factory.
- Each group member is given the results of a customer survey and asked to come up with some ideas to address the issues raised in the survey.
- The group are asked to create a recovery plan after one of the organization's offices was damaged by fire.
- The group are asked to agree a budget for the organization. Each member is briefed about a different department and must argue the case for their department's needs.
- The group are asked to agree the design and space allocation for some new offices. Each represents a particular section and is briefed about the requirements of their section.
- The group are asked to decide how to use a given budget to purchase equipment to allow them to survive if they were stranded in the Arctic.

Practical exercises

As an alternative, or in addition, to role plays, some employers ask candidates to participate in a group activity. As with role play, observers evaluate how the person approaches the task and works with the group. In this case, however, rather than playing a hypothetical role, the candidate is just themselves performing the task. This type of activity is more common in assessments for development purposes than assessment for selection or promotion. Remember that what is being assessed is how participants go about the task – for example, do they help each other, can they agree a strategy, do they get on with other group members – rather than how well they complete the assignment. However, the members of a group that fails completely with the assignment probably haven't performed well.

Examples of tasks might be:

- Agreeing a method to pass a message around the group without speaking or using written notes and successfully using it to transfer messages.
- Making a video to promote a health and safety message.
- Finding materials and making a collage to decorate the staff room.
- Creating a training programme for new staff.
- Using simple equipment to get the team to the other side of the room without touching the floor.
- Building a raft and using it to cross a pond.
- Using planks and ropes to transport some heavy barrels over a high wall.

Objective personality testing

Some personality traits can be measured by looking at the way people complete simple paper and pencil exercises or computer-based tasks. For instance, a person's attention to detail can be determined through a task requiring use of this trait, such as colouring in all the o's in a piece of text. Someone with low attention to detail is likely to miss some of the o's. This approach to measuring personality is sometimes used in providing careers advice, and it can be useful for measuring a limited range of personality traits. It is called 'objective' because rather than asking people to tell you about their personality from their subjective view, the personality information is taken from observing the way they complete a task, and in that sense it is completely objective.

Situational judgement tests

Another type of exercise that is used to elicit a person's behavioural style is called a situational judgement test. In this type of exercise the candidate is presented with a hypothetical situation and asked to choose the option that best reflects how they would respond. These exercises are quite versatile and can be used to measure many things apart from personality traits, but they provide some indication of how a person might behave in a particular situation or how they think it would be appropriate to behave. Situational judgement tests are more likely to be used to measure competencies (see Chapter 4) than pure personality.

These questions may ask you what you *would* do in a particular situation. Some situational judgement test questions focus on what you *should* do – that is, what is the right thing to do in a particular situation – and they are, therefore, less about how you would behave and more about your understanding of what is the correct thing to do. Some questions ask you to choose one best answer. Other formats might ask you to mark the best and worst answers or to rank all the answers from best to worst. Alternatively, you might be asked to rate the answers according to how effective they are.

Some situational judgement test questions have a clear correct answer. More often the best answer will depend on the context. For instance, in the first example below some organizations might prefer people who would speak to John directly. A more hierarchical organization might prefer someone who would refer the matter to a manager. Some situational judgement tests measure personality using options that reflect different personality styles. The third example below is like this. Options 1 and 2 suggest a more people-focused management style, whereas 3 and 4 are typical of a more task-focused one.

Example situational judgement test questions

You could try responding to these questions in the different ways described above, such as rating and ranking the items.

1. You have noticed that John, one of the people who works in your team, is not pulling his weight. He always says he is busy with his own work when anyone asks for his help with a team assignment. How should you deal with this situation?
    1. Explain to John that his behaviour is not fair to the rest of the team.
    2. Speak to your manager about John's attitude.
    3. Take John aside and try to find out why he behaves as he does.
    4. Ignore the situation; it is for your manager to deal with if necessary.

2. A colleague asks you to review a report she has written. It has to be ready tomorrow. You think that although it has some merits it is poorly written and misses out several important topics. How would you deal with this?
    1. Tell her that the report is fine and praise the best parts.
    2. Point out a few errors that need correcting.
    3. Tell her honestly the problems that you see in the report.
    4. Offer to help her correct the report after work.

3. You are appointed as manager of a new department. It is your first day in a new role. Which of the following would you do first?
    1. Call a meeting of the whole team to introduce yourself.
    2. Walk around the department and introduce yourself informally to all the team members you meet.
    3. Ask to be briefed on the main activities and structure of the department.
    4. Arrange a meeting with your manager to hear what is expected from you.

4 What questionnaires measure

In Chapter 2 we looked at what personality is, and it is rather obviously personality that personality questionnaires are designed to measure. However, personality can be interpreted quite broadly to include all those factors that make us different from others. This includes those things that are typically thought of as the core or personality – the way we think, feel and behave, and how we relate to others. More peripheral, but still sometimes included as part of personality, are interests motivations and values. In addition, questionnaires are used to measure emotional intelligence, competencies, leadership style, team types and many other things. Questionnaires measuring these different things can be surprisingly similar, but they can also be very different in style. In this chapter we look at the different areas to be measured, starting with the more mainstream parts of personality and then looking at more specific measurement focuses.

Personality

The core elements of personality can be thought of as a person's behavioural style: how a person interacts with the world. There are hundreds of characteristics that can be listed under this heading, but research suggests that these can be grouped under five broad headings. These are sometimes called the 'big five' personality factors or traits. Some personality questionnaires are designed to measure at this broad level, others look at more specific traits.

Each of the big five traits is conceived as a continuum from one extreme of the trait to the other extreme, and measurements suggest that many people have an intermediate position on the scale between the two extremes. The title of the trait will reflect one of the extremes. Although it could equally be described by an adjective describing the other extreme, a conventional description has developed for four of the five, with descriptors usually at one end. For instance, the extroversion trait is actually the continuum between extreme introversion and extreme extroversion. Most people are somewhere in between the two extremes. The trait could be described as introversion, but convention is to use the term extroversion. We talk about people being *high* on the trait – that is, they have a behavioural style that is typical of the end of the scale used to describe it. Someone who is *low* on the trait will be best described by the opposite of the scale name.

This language is purely conventional. There is no suggestion that it is better to be high on a trait than low. They are purely descriptive of the person's behavioural style. There are no good or bad personality traits. What is true is that certain behavioural styles will be more suitable for certain types of activities – for example, extroverts are better suited to interacting with lots of people, whereas introverts are better at work where there is little opportunity to interact with others.

The descriptions of each of the big five personality traits that follow explain the typical behavioural style of people at the two extremes of each trait, as well as describing what the average person, who is moderate on the trait, may be like. Remember that there are actually very few people who are extreme on any trait and far more who are in the middle or moderately towards one end or the other. As well as a description of the trait there is a short discussion of the types of work that might suit people at different positions on the trait and how they might approach the task of applying for a new job.

You might find that you can place yourself on each of these traits from the descriptions in this chapter. However, you might sometimes find that although some of the description applies to you, some of it does not. This may be because you have a middle position on the trait – you are neither strongly at one extreme nor the other, and so your behaviour is intermediate. Because these are broad traits it could be that you are at one end of a scale for some aspects of the trait and at the other for different aspects. There are some questions at the end of each section to help you decide where you are on the trait.

Openness to experience

High openness

This trait reflects the person's attitude to experiencing and learning about their environment. People who are high on this trait – open to experience – like having new experiences, they are curious about their environment and want to learn more about things. These people tend to be more positive about change. They are often more intellectual and conceptual in their approach to things, wanting to understand and enjoying learning. They may enjoy thinking about abstract concepts or considering hypothetical situations. They tend to be imaginative, have artistic tendencies and be sensitive to beauty. They are likely to be innovative and creative in the way they think and do things. People who are open to experience may easily become bored with routine and crave constant novelty. They may prefer the theoretical over the pragmatic, and this can make them rather impractical.

This sort of behavioural style is appropriate for artistic, creative and intellectual pursuits. It can also be desirable in those involved in research and development. People who are open to experience may be better at coming up with solutions to problems and dealing with constantly changing environments. This style is not suited to performing repetitive or recurring tasks, where things must always be done the same way. People with this personality style may also find it difficult to work in ugly or unattractive situations.

A job seeker with this personality style might be quite creative at finding job opportunities or moulding a CV to particular job requirements. Artistic tendencies could help a person create an attractive CV. Curiosity might spur action to find out more about the employing organization, which could impress an interviewer and help understand what sort of person the organization is looking for.

Someone who is open to experience might be used to thinking about how they approach tasks and be able to give good reflective answers to an interviewer's questions. Creativity could be helpful in providing imaginative responses that are likely to make the candidate more memorable to the interviewer. However, the dull, repetitive side of searching for a job, reading through hundreds of job adverts or filling in yet another similar application form might not appeal to this sort of person, and some interviewers might find unusual responses wacky and unrealistic rather than creative.

Low openness

People who are low on this trait, closed to experience or conformist, take a more straightforward view of things. They prefer the familiar to innovations. They will tend to take things at face value rather than engaging in a lot of analysis or considering alternative possibilities. They may not have a great interest in art or science and will be more concerned with what is happening in the here and now. They tend to be conservative in their approach and may find dealing with change quite difficult. They are often practical and ready to get on with things rather than engaging in a great deal of analysis or searching for alternative approaches.

This behavioural style is suited to coping well with jobs with little in the way of novelty, where the day-to-day tasks may be quite repetitive or where there is little change or variety in the situation or the way things are done. On the other hand, people who are low on openness to experience may be less suited to work requiring the generation of new ideas, where there is a great deal of change and reorganization and where there are no familiar patterns to return to. As a job seeker, someone like this would be less likely to be put off by the dullness of searching through situations vacant listings or filling in yet another similar application form. The lack of curiosity typical of someone low on openness may mean that they neglect to research the company's background because they do not see it as an interesting activity. Answers to the interviewer's questions are likely to be practical and matter of fact rather than creative and original, and people who are low on openness to experience may struggle to analyse their own behaviour for the interviewer.

Moderate openness

People who are intermediate on openness to experience may have a moderate, rather than all-consuming liking for intellectual or creative pursuits, and they may be able to cope with and even welcome some change and variety but find too much change difficult to deal with. They will have a reasonable tolerance of repetition and sameness in aspects of a job and like a balance between the new and the familiar. They may have a degree of imagination and creativity and be able to come up with some new ideas and approaches to problems, but they find it difficult to be creative all the time. They may be better at adapting existing ideas than developing new ones. This balance can mean that they cope well with work that has some elements that do suit those who are open to experience but some elements that suit those with low openness to experience. For instance, copywriters may need to be creative in some parts of their role but may also have to spend much of their time rewriting and checking copy, which can be quite dull.

However, some people who are intermediate on openness to experience may have some of the traits associated with openness but some related to a more closed approach. For example, a person may be very imaginative and creative in their thinking but prefer working in familiar surroundings and dislike dealing with change.

Assess yourself on openness to experience

Circle your answers to the questions below. Are they mostly in the High or Low column? If it is a mixture of both or you find it difficult to decide between the answers you are likely to be moderately open to experience.

	HIGH	LOW
Do you prefer to do something new or something familiar?	New	Familiar
Are you good at coming up with ideas to solve a problem?	Usually	Rarely
Do you prefer the practical or the abstract?	Abstract	Practical
If you don't understand something are you curious to know more or do you tend to let it pass?	Curious	Let it pass

Conscientiousness

High conscientiousness

People who are high on conscientiousness tend to get on with their work well; they are self-disciplined and will keep their word if they say they will do something. They like to finish what they have taken on. They pay attention to details and check the quality and accuracy of their work. They prefer to work in a structured manner and will generally follow rules and guidelines where they exist. This sort of person can be relied on to get on with the job, even when they are not being monitored. They like to plan what they are going to do before embarking on it and may be uncomfortable if this is not possible or if plans are constantly changed. People who are strongly conscientious tend to dislike working in unstructured environments; they may find it frustrating when others do not keep to the rules, put things back in their place and so on or where there is little guidance on how things should be done. They may also dislike working where it is difficult to do things properly, perhaps because of a lack of time or resources. They will feel uncomfortable cutting corners or producing work that is not of the best quality. They dislike working in messy or disorganized environments. They may be quite cautious in their approach and uncomfortable taking risks either in the decisions they take or in the way they do things, and this can mean that they can miss some good opportunities.

It may seem that this sort of behavioural style would be positive for any kind of work, and certainly there is much research that shows that people who are high on conscientiousness will tend to be good employees across many different roles. They will usually get on with their work on their own, and they can be trusted to follow rules and guidelines and to meet deadlines. They generally produce careful, error-free work. A person with this behavioural style is likely to use safety equipment when it is required and to treat an employer's machinery with respect. Because they are focused on their work and they take their responsibilities seriously they are likely to be among the more productive members of a team, making the most of their working time.

However, because of their structured approach to working there are some types of work for which they are less suited. In some jobs a structured approach is less helpful because circumstances are constantly changing and plans become out of date before they are implemented. There are situations where it is necessary to extemporize, to cut corners or to do something quickly, even if it is not perfect. They may find multitasking difficult because they have to move from one thing to another without being able to finish anything properly or tie up loose ends.

A highly conscientious person can become caught up in minor details and lose sight of the main priorities. While it is the role of managers to make sure that other staff are following procedures, they often have to decide when procedures should be abandoned or ignored to meet new priorities. For example, a manager might decide not to check a new delivery according to procedures in order to get the raw materials on to the production line to keep it running or to meet an urgent order. Someone high on conscientiousness might find this kind of decision difficult. People working in sales often need to capitalize on opportunities as they arise, and this may mean abandoning a lead that does not look very promising. This kind of behaviour can make a conscientious person feel uncomfortable.

Highly conscientious people will tend to take a methodical and structured approach to job seeking. They will be careful to meet deadlines for completing application forms and sending in information, and they are likely to turn up to an interview smartly dressed and on time, carrying all the information they need in a neat folder. They will try hard to provide interviewers with the answers to their questions, but they could find that their tendency to focus too much on minor details makes their responses less effective. They may find assessment procedures quite stressful when they do not know what to expect and are unable to prepare themselves appropriately.

Low conscientiousness

People who are low on conscientiousness see deadlines, procedures and work demands as flexible. They prefer not to be constrained by set plans and rules and to be able to respond to the requirements of the moment. They tend to dislike work that requires a meticulous or careful approach. They prefer looking at things in more general, global or 'big picture' terms to getting tied up in detail. They may be more concerned with getting things done and prefer not to spend time checking quality and accuracy. They may become impatient if they are slowed down by someone who wants to do things with greater care and attention. They don't mind taking some risks and are likely to be willing to go with new opportunities that arise even if this means changing plans. They tend to be unstructured in their approach. They can be untidy and messy in their work habits, miss deadlines and fail to finish things properly, leaving loose ends for others to tie up. They may be easily distracted on to other tasks and leave some things undone unless reminded.

Low conscientiousness people are better suited to work in unstructured environments where the focus is on meeting constantly shifting priorities, where it is important to work with the needs of the moment rather than to plan ahead to meet fixed deadlines. They can be suitable for roles where a flexible approach is helpful, such as sales. They can be better at working in multi-tasking or swift-moving environments than people who are high on conscientiousness, but they are not well suited to doing careful, meticulous work, and they may find it difficult to meet deadlines without external prompting and support.

As job seekers, low conscientiousness people will tend to take quite a haphazard approach and often miss opportunities through being late for deadlines or failing to prepare thoroughly. They may arrive late for interviews and forget to bring important documents with them. On the other hand, their natural tendency to extemporize may stand them in good stead when they are dealing with questions they had not expected or exercises they had not prepared for. They are likely to be able to take a broad perspective rather than being distracted by minor details when they are answering an interviewer's questions.

Moderate conscientiousness

People who are intermediate on conscientiousness may be moderately careful and meticulous in their work and place a reasonable degree of importance on meeting standards and deadlines. However, they will not be too rigid in their approach and will balance the need for structure with an understanding of the need to shift priorities to more important tasks and to sometimes leave tasks unfinished. They will be moderately tidy and careful, but they may make errors from time to time or sometimes leave things in a bit of a mess, although they might have a burst of tidying up from time to time.

People with this behavioural style will be well suited to jobs that require a moderate degree of structure and attention to detail. They will also be suitable for jobs that have elements of structured, careful, detailed work as well as elements that require more global thinking or flexible working.

Others who are moderately conscientious may be high on some of the traits associated with conscientiousness and low on others. For example, a person might be very structured and tidy in their work but pay little attention to deadlines and be very willing to restructure what they were doing to meet new priorities. Alternatively, a person might be very risk averse and safety conscious but pay little attention to detail and quality in their work. Depending on which elements of conscientiousness were high and low such people could be suited to roles that required strong conscientiousness in some aspects and low conscientiousness in others.

Assess yourself on conscientiousness

Circle your answers to the questions below. Are they mostly in the High or Low column? If it is a mixture of both you are likely to be moderately conscientious.

	HIGH	LOW
Are you usually early, on time, or late for meetings?	Early or on time	Late
Are you structured or spontaneous?	Structured	Spontaneous
Do you focus on detail or the broad picture?	Detail	Broad picture
Do you find procedures and quality standards helpful guides or a bureaucratic nuisance?	Helpful	Nuisance

Extroversion

High extroversion

Extroversion is one of the best-known personality traits – indeed, the word has entered the general vocabulary. Extroverts are lively and gregarious, and they like to spend time with other people, partying and having fun. However, as well as these better known characteristics, there are some others that are related to extroversion. Extroverts seek excitement and like to be stimulated in all manner of ways. They are often eager for novel experiences, and are the first to want to try out something new. They tend to be quite optimistic in their outlook, which makes them willing to take on new and difficult tasks. They prefer to be in noisy surroundings with lots going on. They like to be the centre of attention and tend to enjoy having an audience to listen to them. They are confident and are rarely reticent about putting themselves forward or singing their own praises. Extroverts may prefer to discuss things with others to thinking things through in their heads. They often want to share their thoughts and feelings with others, and this can lead them unintentionally to say things that are indiscreet or inappropriate on occasion. They make their presence felt in a group and can be quite forceful and assertive. They typically dislike spending time alone, and they may not be good listeners, preferring the sound of their own voice. Their optimism and excitement seeking may mean that they underestimate the risks or difficulties involved in a course of action and take on more than they can deliver.

Extroverts are well suited to roles that require a lot of contact with others, especially jobs where it is important to build rapport with someone quickly, such as many customer service and sales roles. Extroversion is helpful when others need to be motivated or engaged, and this might include positions as team leaders, teachers or trainers and tour guides. It is a positive factor if a role requires much public speaking or influencing and persuading others, and it can also be useful where there are many challenges and it will be necessary to take risks. Extroverts are less well suited to roles where much of the time is spent concentrating and working alone. They are easily distracted, and their need for contact with others may lead them to spend time chatting rather than working. Strong extroverts may sometimes find it hard to be constantly diplomatic and discreet. Equally, they may underestimate the need for caution in some situations.

Extroverts are likely to do well in interviews. They are comfortable meeting new people and are likely to easily strike up a rapport with an interviewer and make a strong impression. They are not shy about talking about themselves and do not tend to suffer from any false modesty about their abilities and achievements. They may sometimes find that their mouth runs away with them and that they give away more than they intended in response to an interviewer's questions. Role plays, presentations and group exercises are also likely to suit the extrovert personality. However, exercises requiring quiet concentration may be more of a challenge, and extroverts may struggle to concentrate on tests and questionnaires or find it hard to focus on completing an application form accurately.

Low extroversion

People who are low on extroversion are described as introverts. These are people who like to balance time spent with others with time on their own. They like to think things through in their heads before sharing their ideas with others. They may find meeting new people difficult or awkward and they prefer to avoid noisy gatherings with many people because they are uncomfortable in such situations and prefer to interact with a few people they know well in less hectic surroundings. They are often quite reserved and would rather be ignored than made the centre of attention. They are more comfortable deferring to others than behaving in an assertive manner, and they may not enjoy influencing or leading others. They tend to be modest and may be reticent about their own skills and achievements or even underrate their capability. They usually keep their feelings to themselves, and others may find them difficult to read. This can make them slow to develop rapport with others and to develop new friendships.

Introverts are particularly suited to roles where there is minimal interaction with others, such as working with machines, tending land or animals, and working with information or computers. In jobs such as driving or operating machinery people spend a great deal of time entirely on their own or with very little opportunity to interact with others, and introverts are much more tolerant than extroverts of this type of work. Introversion may also be a positive trait for jobs that require being with others in a listening rather than a more active role, such as being a counsellor or running focus groups. Introverts can also be good team workers, but they are most comfortable in a low-key role.

Introverts can find the whole process of job seeking quite difficult. Their ability to concentrate alone will help them in completing application forms and collecting information in preparation for a selection day, but they may find the social side of selection more difficult. They may be uncomfortable talking about themselves at interview, and their natural modesty will make it difficult for them to sell themselves effectively. Their natural tendency will be to give short, direct answers to questions, and interviewers may struggle to get them to talk more openly about themselves and their approach to work. Group exercises, requiring interactions with many people, may be particularly difficult, and introverts may find a selection day a tiring experience. However, introverts can learn to present themselves effectively at interview and may show their strengths in written exercises, tests and questionnaires.

Moderate extroversion

The majority of people are neither strong extroverts nor strong introverts. The typical person is mildly to moderately extrovert, and this sort of person may be similar to the extrovert described above, but in a more moderate manner. They like having fun with others and enjoy parties and excitement, but in moderation. They like to balance this type of experience with quieter, more restrained activities. They don't mind being the centre of attention from time to time, but they like to be able to shade into the background sometimes. They are reasonably comfortable meeting new people and establishing rapport but are more comfortable with people they already know. They can cope with spending time alone but like to connect with others when they can.

People who are moderately extrovert are suited to roles that have some elements that require extrovert behaviour and some that do not. For example, someone working in IT maintenance may spend time working directly on computers without human interaction, but another part of the role may involve training users on how to use the system and providing support, which will require contact with people.

Less commonly, some people who are overall moderately extrovert may have some features of a very extrovert behavioural style but not others. For example, someone might be strongly gregarious and prefer lively surroundings but not be very assertive and dislike trying to influence or persuade others. People with these mixed types of behavioural style will be best suited to work that matches their own characteristics.

Assess yourself on extroversion

Circle your answers to the questions below. Are they mostly in the High or Low column? If it is a mixture of both you are likely to be moderately extrovert.

	HIGH	LOW
If you are tired, would you rather spend time on your own or with friends?	With friends	Alone
Are you more of a talker or a listener?	Talker	Listener
Do you enjoy meeting new people?	Yes	No
Do you prefer lively and loud environments or quiet and calm ones?	Lively and loud	Quiet and Calm

Agreeableness

High agreeableness

People who are high on the trait of agreeableness tend to be considerate and helpful in their behaviour. They can be good friends and are often sympathetic listeners, and they will try to help others with their problems and concerns and are concerned for the welfare of others. They prefer cooperation to competition when they are working with others and will generally like working in teams. They tend to be trusting and tolerant of others and are not easily irritated by other people's behaviour. They may, however, find it difficult to keep a professional distance and become too involved in other people's problems. They tend to dislike and avoid conflict and will try to smooth over disagreements between others. Their dislike of conflict can make it difficult for people with this behavioural style to deliver bad news or to challenge other people's behaviour or opinions, and they can be too gullible and easily taken in by other people.

People with this behavioural style can be good in situations where helpfulness and sympathetic listening are required. Suitable positions include some of the caring professions as well as the service industry, such as customer care. However, highly agreeable people will struggle with roles that are competitive or that involve conflict. Roles where there is a recurring need to be assertive with others, such as dealing with difficult customers, enforcing performance and quality standards, and selling and negotiating on behalf of an organization, could be a problem, and people who are too agreeable may have difficulty with staff management roles for this reason. They may find it difficult to maintain an emotional separation from people they work with, and where this happens it can lead to burn-out in caring rules.

Agreeable people will be accommodating as job seekers. They will try hard to meet the needs of the employer, such as being available for interview when it suits the recruiting organization. Their cooperative and helpful attitude may be appreciated by an interviewer, but their dislike of conflict will tend to make them less effective when it comes to negotiating terms and conditions or salary. Where agreeableness is a positive factor for the job they are likely to come across well in interpersonal exercises such as role plays. However, they may find competing with other candidates in a group exercise more difficult.

Low agreeableness

People who are low on the trait of agreeableness are more selective in their sympathies and support for others. They may be quite competitive in their approach to many situations and generally consider their own, or their department's or organization's, needs before others. They will tend to invest energy in getting the best outcome from situations for themselves and those with whom they identify. They are likely to be independent thinkers and to take quite a sceptical approach to what they see and hear. They may question other people's motives and intentions rather than taking them on trust, which means that they are unlikely to be taken in. When there is a difference of opinion they will express their own view and try to influence others to their way of thinking. They will not shirk from delivering bad news or expressing views that may be controversial.

Someone who is low on the agreeableness trait will be suited to work in a competitive environment or where straight talking is required. This could include many roles in sales and where there is the cut and thrust of business competition. They will generally be able to maintain a professional distance and not become emotionally involved in other people's problems. They may be suited to roles where standards or policies need to be enforced, such as roles in security or managing difficult people. However, their general lack of empathy may mean that they lack insight into other people's problems and ride roughshod over their feelings.

The competitiveness typical of low agreeableness people may stand them in good stead as job candidates. It may give them the extra drive needed to put some effort into preparation for job interviews and to present themselves effectively on the day. They need to be careful not to behave too aggressively with interviewers, but their assertiveness may help them stand out from the other candidates and negotiate a good deal if they are offered the job.

Moderate agreeableness

People who are intermediate on agreeableness will be generally sympathetic and supportive of others but will be more easily able to maintain an emotional distance from other people's problems than those who are high on the trait. They will be willing to help others but will balance this with meeting their own personal needs. They are likely to have the flexibility to work in both cooperative and competitive modes without being extremely competitive or extremely compliant. Although they may not enjoy giving unpleasant messages, they will face up to doing it when necessary. They will express their own views in a discussion but will also listen to what others have to say and be ready to be persuaded by a stronger view.

A moderately agreeable behavioural style is suitable for many types of work because people like this will be comfortable working cooperatively or competitively. They can deal sympathetically with other people but can also maintain sufficient professional distance not to become inappropriately emotionally involved in their problems.

Others who are moderate on agreeableness may have some of the traits of agreeableness very strongly but be at the non-agreeableness end of the spectrum on others. For example, a person might be trusting of others but not sympathetic to their difficulties. Another person might be caring and cooperative in their approach but rather low on trust and be wary and suspicious of others.

In terms of suitability for different types of work, the behavioural style of this sort of person needs to be matched to the job requirements. It will depend on the exact nature of the job and the behavioural style of the individual.

Assess yourself on agreeableness

Circle your answers to the questions below. Are they mostly in the High or Low column? If it is a mixture of both you are likely to be moderately agreeable.

	HIGH	LOW
Do you go out of your way to help others?	Yes	No
Are you trusting of people or are you wary of others?	Trusting	Wary
Do you have quite a competitive streak?	No	Yes
Are you soft and sympathetic when people have problems or tough-minded and expect them to sort themselves out?	Soft and sympathetic	Tough-minded

Emotional stability

High emotional stability

People with high emotional stability tend to have a relaxed and laid-back approach to life. They are not easily upset by people and events and tend to be able to take life's problems in their stride. They are likely to be quite confident and optimistic in their outlook and not anticipate problems before they have happened. They tend to be quite thick-skinned, brushing off criticism and insults from others, and they can be quite insensitive to others. They are difficult to anger and can cope well with pressure without becoming nervous or anxious. They are less likely than others to get worked up before important events. Sometimes their calm approach to things may mean that they do not become sufficiently energized to deal with a crisis or pressurized situation, and this behaviour can seem like a lack of interest or motivation.

People with this behavioural style are well suited to dealing with stressful jobs. They can keep calm in a crisis and keep functioning without panicking. This is appropriate for jobs requiring crisis management skills or working in a pressurized environment. They can cope with having to make difficult decisions and will also be able to deal with adverse criticism without becoming unduly upset or taking things personally. This is helpful for roles where people deal with complaints and problems for much of the time. However, their approach may be too relaxed for some roles because they may not take problems or issues sufficiently seriously and not invest energy in finding solutions and dealing with matters.

As job seekers their laid-back approach will mean that they do not suffer too much from nerves when attending interviews or completing tests and exercises. Their calm and together approach is likely to impress an interviewer, but their lack of nerves may mean that they fail to reach their full potential at interviews because a little bit of anxiety can be helpful in spurring performance.

Low emotional stability

People who are low on emotional stability tend to be quite anxious and tense. They find it difficult to relax and switch off, and they may find themselves continually worrying about things. They can become quite agitated before important events, and this can lead to poor performance. They can be pessimistic in outlook and anticipate difficulties and problems before they arise, which can lead them to be indecisive or overly cautious in their approach. They are sensitive to criticism and can be easily upset by the remarks of others. This may exacerbate their feelings of tension, and they may be easily irritated or angered. They can sometimes misinterpret innocuously intended remarks as critical and react accordingly.

Their nervous energy can be helpful in motivating them to get on with things and make them more vigorous in trying to achieve their goals. However, their highly anxious approach can come across as neurotic and difficult. They may be difficult to manage, not least because their oversensitivity to chance remarks makes them touchy and demanding.

They may find it difficult to calm down or switch off from outside pressures when they are at work and from work pressures when they are at home.

The nervous energy of low emotional stability can be a source of motivational force to invest in tasks. Such people may be able to harness this nervous energy positively in a crisis to help increase their effort and surmount difficulties, and they sometimes have a strong need to achieve or to produce high quality results. They may work hard to deal with anticipated problems and to calm their own nerves. However, their oversensitivity makes them unsuitable for jobs where they are likely to face much criticism and do not have a supportive manager. Their general level of anxiety may make them susceptible to stress-related conditions.

The high anxiety levels of someone low on emotional stability will mean that interviews for new jobs can be very difficult. People like this may not perform at their best because of nerves, and interviewers may pick up on this. A sympathetic interviewer may do their best to calm the candidate down, but someone less sympathetic could become impatient, which could make the situation even worse. A pessimistic outlook will not help because the candidate's expectations that something will go wrong will only increase their nervousness. There are many techniques that people who do tend to get nervous can use to calm themselves down before important events, and it is worth spending time mastering one or two of these if you do suffer from nerves. Many people, for example, find concentrating on calm, even breathing for a minute or two very effective.

Moderate emotional stability

Those who have an intermediate level of emotional stability will tend to be reasonably relaxed for the most part, although they may be susceptible to nerves before important events or when they are approaching deadlines or important milestones in projects. This nervous energy may be helpful in achieving peak performance under pressure, and they may, therefore, be able to channel their anxiety positively for the most part but also be able to relax and calm down after difficult periods. They are likely to be able to balance a realistic view of the potential success of a project with a pragmatic understanding of the possible problems and pitfalls that could arise. Although they will not be indifferent to how they are seen by others, they will not be overly sensitive to criticism and should generally be able to take it in their stride and learn from constructive comments.

Other people who are moderate in emotional stability may, on the other hand, have some of the traits associated with emotional stability and some that are more related to the more neurotic end of the trait. They may, for example, be highly anxious, find it difficult to relax, be generally irritable and easy to anger, but on the whole they may be quite thick-skinned and not worried by the criticism or comments of others.

Assess yourself on emotional stability

Circle your answers to the questions below. Are they mostly in the High or Low column? If it is a mixture of both you are likely to be moderately emotionally stable.

	HIGH	LOW
Do you worry a lot?	No	Yes
Are you generally optimistic or pessimistic?	Optimistic	Pessimistic
Do you take decisions easily or worry about them a lot?	Easily	Worry
Are you confident and relaxed or tense and stressed?	Confident and relaxed	Tense and stressed

Competencies

Competencies are similar to personality traits in some ways but rather than trying to explain how people think, feel and behave in a general way, competencies focus on a person's ability to do a job or at least some aspect of it. Competencies are often related to one or more personality traits but may also require relevant skills, abilities and knowledge. A person with a competency has those characteristics that result in effective job performance. An example of a competency might be problem solving, which is something you might have to do in many jobs. To be good at this you need to be good at analysing situations, but you also need to be quite creative to see the problem from different perspectives and come up with some ideas for solutions. If you had learned some problem-solving techniques this might also help improve your problem-solving competency.

Another example of a competency is team working, which requires a different set of characteristics. In this case they would be mostly personality characteristics. A good team worker relates well to others in the team and is willing to help other team members. They will also work hard to help complete the team's tasks and activities rather than leaving it to others to do the work. In term of the 'big five' personality dimensions discussed above, a good team worker needs to be moderate or above on agreeableness and moderate or above on conscientiousness. It would, therefore, be possible to use personality questionnaire scores to learn about some of a person's competencies, and many employers do this with personality questionnaires. However, some employers prefer to measure competencies directly through questionnaires. These questionnaires may look like personality questionnaires, but the questions will be more focused on working effectively than on your style of working.

Unlike personality traits, where there are no good or bad scores, competencies are directly about effectiveness at work, and so it is better to be high on a competency than low. However, it is the nature of competencies that some of them are not compatible with others – that is, if you are high on one you are unlikely to be high on another. For example, someone who is good at planning and organizing is less likely to be good at adapting to change and vice versa. The very traits that make you good at one tend to interfere with the other.

Also in contrast to personality, there is no consensus on competency models. Typically, each organization develops its own set of competencies, and sometimes each role has its own series of competencies. In addition, competencies with similar titles can be quite different in different competency models. One organization might focus their leadership competency on setting objectives and managing work, for example, whereas another might focus more on the interpersonal aspects of leadership, such as energizing and motivating a team.

Following are descriptions of some typical competencies and some questions that might be used to measure them. You will see that these questions are quite transparent, and it would be easy to paint a very rosy picture of your competencies. For this reason these questionnaires are not often used for selection but to aid in personal development. In this context a 360-degrees approach is often used. This is where as well as completing a questionnaire yourself, others who know you well and work with you, such as your manager, several colleagues and the people who report to you, could all be asked to complete questionnaires. Customers and clients are also sometimes asked to complete the questionnaire. In this way an all-round perspective on your competence, reflecting different views of your performance, is gained.

Where a competency approach is used in selection you may find that rather than rating individual items you are asked to choose which statement from a number drawn from different competencies is most true of you – that is, you have to say which your strongest competencies are. Some competency questionnaires ask you to rate your agreement with statements or say how true they are of you. Others might ask you to rate how frequently you do something. The examples below use different formats so that you can practise different response options.

Don't worry if you don't have all these competencies. Most people are competent in a number of areas, but few, if any, people are competent in all areas. Employers know this and focus on the competencies that are most important for the role they are selecting for. For instance, drive and initiative is not a requirement in all roles. Where managers and supervisors set policy and deal with problems, other staff do not need to show much initiative. If the role does not require it, someone with strong drive and initiative might become frustrated and unhappy. However, competencies are a useful way of thinking about your particular strengths – what you can bring to a role. Equally, if there is a competency that you don't have a great deal of but that is important for the work you would like to do, you could identify this as a development need for yourself. Although your personality is fairly fixed and difficult to change, competencies can be developed.

Drive and initiative

People who are high on this competency are good at making things happen. They don't wait to be told what to do; rather they see what needs to be done and go and do it. They have energy and initiative and are self-motivated. They are willing to take decisions where needed to make things happen and will act on opportunities when they arise.

Example drive and initiative questions

Rate how frequently you do each of the following at work using the scale below.

1	2	3	4	5
Rarely	Occasionally	Sometimes	Often	Nearly always

	RESPONSE
I use my own initiative when something needs doing.	
I can make decisions on partial information if necessary.	
I make sure I achieve my objective at work.	

Adapting to change

People who are high on this competency cope well with change. If their priorities are changed or the organization restructures, they adapt flexibly and quickly to the new circumstances. They don't get upset but keep on working as effectively as they can. They don't become stressed under pressure or in a crisis but remain composed and focused on their work.

Example adapting to change questions

Rate the extent to which you agree with each of the following statements using the scale below.

1	2	3	4	5
Strongly disagree	Disagree	Neither agree nor disagree	Agree	Strongly agree

RESPONSE

I am calm in a crisis.	
I cope well with change.	
I have a flexible approach to my work.	

Influencing

People who are good at influencing have the ability to gain people's agreement to their proposals. This might be in the context of getting a team to accept a new way of working or selling a product to a client. They can present ideas effectively and adapt their message to the needs of others. They are good negotiators.

Example influencing questions

Rate the extent to which you agree with each of the following statements using the scale below.

1	2	3	4	5
Strongly disagree	Disagree	Neither agree nor disagree	Agree	Strongly agree

RESPONSE

I can easily persuade others.	
I am good at selling.	
I negotiate effectively.	

Communication

People who are good at communication can express themselves clearly either in writing or orally. They have a clear, effective style and understand the needs of the listener or reader. They will check that their message is understood and adapt it if necessary to the recipient.

Example communication questions

Rate how frequently you do each of the following at work using the scale below.

1	2	3	4	5
Rarely	Occasionally	Sometimes	Often	Nearly always

RESPONSE

I take account of my audience when presenting.	
I write effective reports.	
I explain complex information straightforwardly.	

Managing tasks

People who are good at managing tasks can plan and organize well. They set clear goals, establish priorities and monitor progress to make sure that things get done. They make sure that deadlines are met and monitor standards. They work in an organized manner.

Example managing tasks questions

Rate how frequently you do each of the following at work using the scale below.

1	2	3	4	5
Rarely	Occasionally	Sometimes	Often	Nearly always

RESPONSE

	RESPONSE
I take time to organize my work before I start.	
I get things done on time and within budget.	
I make sure that quality standards are maintained.	

Problem solving

People who are good at problem solving can collect and analyse information about people or situations. This may include interpreting data as well as verbal and visual information. They can see to the core of a problem and focus on the most important issues. They find practical and rational solutions that are simple and effective.

Example problem solving questions

Rate the extent to which you agree with each of the following statements using the scale below.

1	2	3	4	5
Strongly disagree	Disagree	Neither agree nor disagree	Agree	Strongly agree

RESPONSE

I am good at analysing data.	
I can find practical solutions to problems.	
I understand complex information.	

Innovating

People who are good at innovating can easily generate ideas and options. As well as developing their own ideas and solutions to problems, they can build creatively on the ideas of others. They can see the possibilities in a situation and develop new opportunities. They often come up with ideas others haven't thought of.

Example innovating questions

Rate how frequently you do each of the following at work using the scale below.

1	2	3	4	5
Rarely	Occasionally	Sometimes	Often	Nearly always

RESPONSE

Others come to me for ideas.	
I can think up several different ways of solving a problem.	
I can adapt my ideas for different situations.	

Strategic thinking

People who have a good strategic perspective look at issues in a broad context and see the relationships between different parts of a business or organization. They can see the implications of decisions across a wide range of functions and over a longer time scale. They look beyond their own day-to-day responsibilities to take a broader perspective.

Example strategic thinking questions

Rate the extent to which you agree with each of the following statements using the scale below.

1	2	3	4	5
Strongly disagree	Disagree	Neither agree nor disagree	Agree	Strongly agree

	RESPONSE
I take a strategic view of issues.	
I understand problems from a broad perspective.	
I take a long term view.	

Team working

Good team workers work well with others, contributing towards achieving the common goal. They will support and help others to improve the team's performance, and they are cooperative and will give way to the team consensus if others do not agree with them.

Example team working questions

Rate how frequently you do each of the following at work using the scale below.

1	2	3	4	5
Rarely	Occasionally	Sometimes	Often	Nearly always

RESPONSE

	RESPONSE
I work well in a team.	
I help others when they need it.	
I encourage others to express their views.	

Leadership

Good leaders inspire and motivate others to work towards organizational goals. They can create and share a vision for the future and generate enthusiasm in others to achieve it. They relate well to others and are well respected by them. They encourage others to give of their best.

Example leadership questions

Rate how frequently you do each of the following at work using the scale below.

1	2	3	4	5
Rarely	Occasionally	Sometimes	Often	Nearly always

RESPONSE

	RESPONSE
Others will follow my lead.	
I treat others with dignity and respect.	
I celebrate the achievements of others.	

Example competency comparison questions

For each set of four statements choose the one that is most like you and the one that is least like you.

	MOST LIKE ME	LEAST LIKE ME
I use my own initiative when something needs doing.		
I am calm in a crisis.		
I negotiate effectively.		
I write clearly.		

I get things done on time and within budget.		
I am good at analysing data.		
I can adapt my ideas for different situations.		
I take a strategic view of issues.		

I help others when they need it.		
Others will follow my lead.		
I'm an effective presenter.		
I make quick decisions.		

Emotional intelligence

In recent years the concept of emotional intelligence has become popular within the business world. It was popularized in a book by Daniel

Goleman in the mid-1990s. The idea is that there is a parallel between intelligence in terms of thinking skills, which allows people to work well with information, and the ability to work well with people, which is seen as work in the emotional domain. It is certainly the case that there are people who are very bright in conventional terms but who do not seem to perform well in work roles. Equally, there are people with only moderate intelligence who are very successful. We have already looked at the importance of personality in promoting effective working, and it could certainly be argued that ability without an appropriate behavioural style might not be effective. The idea of emotional intelligence goes further by arguing that it is specific aspects of behaviour and understanding of the self and others that are necessary for effective performance.

Emotional intelligence is defined as the capacity to identify and understand your own emotions and feelings and those of others and use this awareness to guide your thinking and actions to promote overall effectiveness – that is, people who are emotionally intelligent are aware of their own feelings and also those of others in a given situation. They understand how these feelings affect the situation and will take them into account in what they do, and they use this understanding to bring the best out of people. Consider, for example, a shop assistant who is dealing with a customer who is angry because an order he placed has not arrived. If the shop assistant is emotionally intelligent she will realize that the customer is angry about the order and will have insight into her own feelings in dealing with the customer. Perhaps she is feeling frightened or upset at the customer's behaviour. She will consider whether it would be better to let the customer see how she is feeling or to hide her emotions and remain calm. She would know how to control her own emotions if necessary and would act to manage the customer's emotions. She might, for instance, let him vent his anger for a little while before trying to calm him because she understands that he needs an outlet for his emotion. She might then try to find a constructive solution that would be acceptable to him.

There is some controversy about these ideas among academics, and also about how emotional intelligence should be measured. Some argue that it is not possible to measure it by way of self-report questionnaires and that it needs to be assessed through external assessment e.g. by people who know you well. Some see emotional intelligence as part of a person's personality and others as behaviours that can be learned and therefore more akin to competencies. This is also reflected in measures of emotional intelligence which can be more like personality questionnaires or more like competency questionnaires. Some measures of emotional intelligence focus relatively narrowly on the areas contained within the definition. Others take a broader view and include competencies or personality traits which are more peripheral to the core definition.

A typical emotional intelligence questionnaire might measure 5 or 6 domains or scales. The following areas are likely to be covered in a measure of emotional intelligence.

- Self-awareness – This is the extent to which you are aware of your own emotional states and moods and how they affect the way you think and feel. Our emotions can affect the way we evaluate the world. Someone with self-awareness realizes the difference between not enjoying a film because it is bad and not enjoying a film because they are in a bad mood.
- Self-control – This is the ability to keep your emotions and moods in check and to control impulses. It allows you to manage your behaviour and stay composed and positive, even if you are feeling upset or distressed.
- Social skills – There are a number of factors under this heading. First, the ability to recognize the emotions and motivations of others. Second, the capacity to take their emotions into account when interacting with others. Third, the capacity to build and maintain good relationships with others.
- Empathy – This is the ability to understand what other people are feeling and see things from their perspective. This is more than just recognizing an emotion – seeing that the person is angry, for example. It is appreciating why the person might be angry in that situation – for example, how frustrating it must be to have to make another trip to collect an order.
- Motivation – This is the enthusiasm and persistence to keep working towards your goals and to maintain effort in the face of potential failure. An optimistic outlook helps to prevent emotionally intelligent people from giving up too early and to counter feelings of hopelessness or despair.

Motivation, values and interests

Motivation, values and interests can be thought of as part of personality or as separate concepts. Elements of motivation, values and interests are often included within personality questionnaires – for instance, an important motivator for many people is the need for achievement, and achievement orientation is often a scale in personality questionnaires. Within the 'big five' model of personality it is usually thought of as part of conscientiousness. Several personality questionnaires have scales that look at your interest in art and culture (part of openness to experience). However, there is value in looking at these areas separately and in more detail, and there are questionnaires that focus on each of these.

Motivation

Motivation concerns what drives you to invest energy in things (to work at them), and questionnaires seek to identify what are the strongest motivators and demotivators for you – that is, what is important to you in your work life and what you would try to avoid. For instance, for some people an element of competition is an excellent driver. They are energized when there is an opportunity to compete with another person, team or company. This could be through trying to reach the highest sales figures, make the fewest errors, have the highest customer ratings or produce the most product. This type of person would probably not put in that extra effort if there were no way of comparing their performance against that of others. For other people, however, competition is not a motivator. They might even be put off by a competitive spirit among other workers and find it difficult to get excited by competition. This could lead them to invest less effort in their work because they didn't want to compete.

If a person's motivators match the job and organizational environment they are likely to work harder in the job and enjoy it more. If there is a mismatch between a person's motivators and the job or organization, the person is less likely to work hard through lack of motivation, and indeed they may be more likely to leave and seek work elsewhere. For this reason the employer using a motivation questionnaire might be most interested in what might demotivate you or turn you off. As with a personality questionnaire, the employer might want to discuss these with you at interview and understand the implications if you were to take up the job. Equally, you would be unlikely to want to take a job that you found demotivating, unless, of course, there were some strong motivators associated with the work as well.

Motivation questionnaires typically have between 10 and 20 scales. They are likely to follow one of the formats used for personality questionnaires, although you could be asked to rate how important something is to you or how it affects your motivation rather than whether you agree with a statement. Some common motivators that are likely to be included in a motivation questionnaire are described below.

Achievement
People with a strong need for achievement like to have something to strive for. They get a kick out of making their targets and objectives. They can feel demotivated if they have nothing to achieve. The more challenging the target the more motivating it is, although targets that people perceive as impossible do not usually have motivating power.

Power
People with a high need for power enjoy being in control, having responsibility and being able to set the direction. They are likely to be quite unhappy if they are not consulted in decision making or are countermanded or ignored.

Affiliation
People with this need want to have warm relationships with people. They will be motivated by working with friendly others and be demotivated by work that is too much alone or in circumstances where there are disagreements and conflict.

Competition

People who are motivated by competition define their goals in terms of doing better than others. They like to win, and it is the effort they put in to be the best that makes them work hard. They may be demotivated in highly cooperative environments where there is no one to compete with. People who are low on this motivation may prefer to work in a cooperative manner and dislike, and can be demotivated by, competitive environments.

Autonomy

People who are motivated by autonomy want to be independent and set their own course. They dislike being told what to do and find being closely managed demotivating. There are also people who find autonomy demotivating. They feel more comfortable being given clear instructions on what to do and having a supportive supervisor.

Recognition

Most people find recognition of their contribution and achievements motivating. They work better when they feel that what they do is appreciated. However, for some people this is a very strong need, and they may become demotivated and insecure if they are ignored or constantly criticized.

Interest

For some people the most important motivator is doing something they find stimulating or interesting. This is an intrinsic motivator because it is the nature of the work that is interesting. Just doing the work provides the motivation. These people may have little tolerance for dull or repetitive work and find it demotivating. People with a low need for interest are better suited to this type of work.

Growth

People with a need for growth get a buzz from developing their own skills and learning. They will enjoy work that stretches them in new areas or requires them to master new skills. They may be demotivated by unchallenging work that is easily within their capacity.

Reward

For some people it is the extrinsic rewards from work that are most important. Key among these is monetary reward. Knowing that their work is directly connected to what they are paid – through bonuses, pay rises or commission – is motivating. They will put in more effort to earn more. For some people being paid well is a form of recognition. For other people money is much less important, as long as they can pay the bills.

Values

Our values reflect what we think is a desirable state. For example, a person might think that it is good for people to express their emotions openly – sharing feelings is something that that person values – but another person might think that it is better for people to keep their emotions to themselves, particularly in work situations. This second person values rational, rather than emotional interaction with others.

Values are often more strongly related to the type of environment we like than to the work we can do, and they are therefore used to provide an indication of how a person might fit with the organization and its culture rather than the work itself. Someone who values cooperation may not be happy in a competitive environment, and a person who values getting things right or the quality of produce would prefer to work in an organization with similar values rather than one that valued quantity and turnover.

There is some overlap between motivation and values, but whereas motivation focuses on the drive to perform, values focus on feelings about what is and is not desirable. However, if you think it is a good thing for people to achieve difficult objectives you will probably be motivated by having a challenging target to achieve. Because of this overlap the content of values questionnaires is often quite similar to measures of motivation.

Interests

Interests are very much what the name suggests. Different people have different interests: some like train spotting, some find people watching fascinating, some enjoy working with their hands, and some people just like to be outdoors. Interest measures are most often used in career counselling to understand what areas of work might appeal to a person. They typically ask about different types of tasks, such as organizing information, helping people with problems, mending things and so on, and from your results on the questionnaire, you will often receive a list of careers that match your interests.

Interest domains are often related to personality domains. For instance, an interest in helping or caring for people is typically related to the personality dimension of agreeableness. A common model used in interest inventories is one developed by US psychologist John L. Holland, and this divides people into six major types in terms of their career interests. These are described below.

Realistic, practical
People with this interest type like working with their hands, using tools and machinery or doing physical work or sports. Related jobs include driver, optician, plumber, radiologist and fire fighter.

Investigative
Investigative types like working with ideas rather than things. They enjoy learning, exploring, researching and trying to solve intellectual problems. Related jobs include biologist, historian, academic, doctor and researcher.

Artistic
The artistic type enjoys expressive creative activities, such as performing, designing and writing. They like opportunities to use their imagination and express their feelings. Relevant jobs include artist, designer, graphic designer, copywriter, writer and photographer.

Social
People belonging to this type are interested in promoting the welfare of others. They like interacting with people to help, teach or serve them. Related jobs include teacher, nurse, care assistant, therapist and customer service officer.

Enterprising

People with this interest type like leading, managing and organizing. They enjoy influencing others and working towards ambitious goals. Typical jobs for this type are manager, entrepreneur, sales person, marketing executive and shopkeeper.

Conventional

Conventional interest types prefer to work with information and data. They like exploring numbers, organizing information and work that requires attention to detail. Typical jobs for this type are administrator, accountant, librarian, office manager, bookkeeper and computer programmer.

Work styles

Some questionnaires are based on a more functional approach. They look at an aspect of work, such as leadership or working in a team, and try to determine a person's style of doing these things. In addition, information on work styles may be derived from more general questionnaires. Detailed personality questionnaires often allow this sort of analysis, and you may be told that the questionnaire is profiling your team type or your learning style.

Some of the specific work style questionnaires are similar in style to personality questionnaires. Others are more like a competency questionnaire and can even take a 360-degree approach (see page 68). For instance, measurement of leadership style may take this approach.

For each area of work there are many different models – far too many to list here – that might be measured, but below are some examples of these types of model to give you an idea of the sort of information they provide.

Team types

Meredith Belbin developed one model of how people work in teams. He suggested that there are a number of roles that people can take in a team, and depending on the work of the team different roles are required.

Belbin's research suggested that for complex tasks teams in which a wide range of roles are represented often produce the best results. Understanding the roles that you are comfortable taking in a team can help you work better with others, and the whole team can better understand its strengths and weaknesses through an analysis of the roles team members typically take. For example, if a team has too many people who want to lead and direct the work there could be conflict. On the other hand, if no one takes this role the team may be without direction.

Below is a short description of the team types that Belbin developed.

Team role	Description
Coordinator	Acts as chairperson, coordinates action; can be manipulative.
Shaper	Energetic, drives others forward; may be insensitive to others' needs.
Implementer	Well-organized and practical; wants to get things done; can be inflexible.
Completer/finisher	Conscientious; checks detail; can be a worrier and poor at delegating.
Plant	Comes up with ideas for the team; may be impractical and less involved in getting work done.
Monitor/evaluator	Reviews what is happening and flags when there may be problems; may seem negative and critical.
Specialist	Has or develops expertise in key areas.
Team worker	Cooperative; cares for team members and tries to smooth relationships in the team.
Resource/investigator	Good networker; can pull in useful resources for the team; can be too optimistic.

Leadership styles

There is something of a growth industry in developing models of leadership. Many different models are used, and different models fit different purposes. Many of these models are quite complex, and they may have a great deal of overlap with personality domains. A simpler model that is frequently used looks at how much a person focuses on making sure things get done (the task) and how much on the people being led.

LEADERSHIP STYLE

HIGH	Leader creates a comfortable and friendly environment; people are cared for but there is little direction and work output may be poor; turnover is likely to be low also.	Balanced approach; provides direction and shows concern for individuals; consultative approach to decision making; output is high and turnover is low.
LOW	Leader does as little as possible; relies on the team to do the work, with little investment in the team or providing direction; output may be low and turnover high.	Focused leader who provides direction; authoritarian approach with little concern for people; output is good but turnover may be high.

FOCUS ON PEOPLE (left axis)

LOW   HIGH

FOCUS ON TASK

Selling styles

There are many models of selling styles, but they generally focus on how someone might go about selling rather than whether they can actually sell. Below are some examples of selling style types.

Selling style	Description
Relationship based	Is sociable and friendly; relates well to others and develops trust with clients; is emotionally aware; sells through personal relationships.
Information based	Analyses customer needs and understands products well; good style for complex product lines; rational approach.
Energy based	Uses enthusiasm and drive to make sales; is confident and persuasive.

Dark side

There has been some interest recently on what has been termed the 'dark side' of personality. This involves looking at how people who have quite extreme personality traits behave. Extreme personality traits are very unusual, and only a very small percentage of the population is at the extreme. However, the impact of an extreme personality trait on a person's behaviour could be critical. In certain circumstances, it is argued, behaviour of those at the extremes of some traits can become difficult and dysfunctional. Someone who is low on trusting could be described as shrewd, and being shrewd is a positive quality in many circumstances: shrewd people are unlikely to be taken in easily, they take a critical view of information they are given, and they check out people and assumptions rather than taking them at face value. A shrewd, astute police officer, for instance, would probably be more effective than a trusting but gullible one.

However, shrewdness in the extreme can turn into suspicious mistrust. A high degree of mistrust might be debilitating, and assuming that all information is invalid and nobody's intentions are what they seem could lead to paranoia and an inability to function. There would be particular concern if a manager showed these tendencies in supervising staff. To work for someone who didn't trust you at all would be very difficult. A mistrustful manager might not share important information with subordinates, thereby preventing them from working effectively. The manager might also be overly critical of others and undermine their motivation by constantly challenging their intentions.

Dark side questionnaires concentrate on identifying extreme tendencies in people's personalities rather than on understanding behaviour that is more usually seen. They are usually used only for senior positions, where the negative behaviours could be most harmful and most difficult to manage. They are sometimes used in selection but more often in development activities to help managers become aware of any dysfunctional tendencies they may have.

Unlike other personality questionnaires, the inference from dark side measures is that some personalities are undesirable. That said, it is not claimed that all people with extreme scores show negative behaviours. Rather, there is the potential for negative behaviour to develop in people identified as belonging to an extreme group.

5 How employers use personality questionnaires

There are a number of ways in which an employer might use a questionnaire as part of a selection exercise. They might use the questionnaire in a relatively early stage of the selection process to eliminate highly unsuitable candidates, or they might choose to use it later in the process to provide quite detailed information about individuals to support the final decision. Equally, the employer might use the questionnaire to apply quite simple selection rules – to include people who have scores in a certain region of one or more scales and to reject people who have scores in other regions of some scales. Alternatively, the employer might use the questionnaire in a more qualitative manner to understand the typical behaviour of a person. In this case they will often use the outcome of the personality questionnaire as the basis for some interview questions to verify the results and elicit more details. We will discuss these different ways of using personality profiles in more detail.

Before a personality questionnaire can be used effectively, information about the role and the role requirements must be collected, and there are a number of ways that this can be done. Questionnaires designed for this purpose can be used, although more usually a description of the role requirements will be developed through structured interviews with relevant people. The manager in charge of the role and also sometimes senior managers, other people who work in the same role is nearly always interviewed and people who work with those in the role. This process is called job analysis.

Once a good understanding of the requirements of the role has been developed it can be used to understand the implications for personality. For example, if the role requires frequently dealing with conflict the person will need to be reasonably confident and able to develop relationships with others. If it is critical that no errors are made someone with good attention to detail is required. For any role there will usually be a few clear personality indications that can be used to select people, but there will generally be several areas of personality for which there are no specific requirements. This means that an employer will not be looking for a specific personality profile but rather focusing on a few critical areas.

Early in the selection process the focus of the employer is on weeding out unsuitable applicants. The idea is to create a shortlist of candidates who will be assessed at the next stage in more detail through one or more interviews and exercises. At later stages the focus changes to finding the most suitable candidates. In using a personality measure to deselect people who are unsuitable, employers will be looking at aspects of personality that relate strongly to major elements of the role. For example, someone who was strongly introverted would find a sales role, which requires constant contact with customers to develop and maintain relationships, to understand their needs and to persuade them to buy more, difficult. Someone who prefers to spend time on their own and is shy and retiring will find it hard to relate well to people in the manner required in sales. The employer might use a personality questionnaire to sift out applicants like this. Another example might be a clerical role, where an important part of the job is to proof-read documents for errors. This requires good concentration, attention to detail and a capacity to tolerate repetitive tasks. People who seek excitement and tend to look at the big picture rather than focusing on detail would be unsuitable for this sort of role, and using a questionnaire could sift them out early in the selection process.

At this stage it is most likely that the employer is looking at only a few aspects of behaviour strongly related to the job and is only sifting out people who are extremely different from the desired behavioural style. Often these decisions will be based on previous research that shows how personality results relate to job performance. It is unlikely that the employer will want to talk to you about your profile at this stage, although they may be willing to provide some feedback to you on your results.

When a personality questionnaire is used at a later stage of selection there are two main ways in which the information is used. One is similar in some ways to the early shortlisting use of the questionnaire, but the employer may be interested in more aspects of personality. In previous examples we saw that a highly introverted person would not be suitable in sales and a highly excitement seeking person would not be suitable for close, detailed work. At the next stage the employer might consider the degree of extroversion or excitement seeking of the individual as one aspect of the individual's job suitability. The individual is assessed not simply by looking at some scores as suitable and others as not suitable. Rather, there will be an assessment of how suitable the person is. The more extrovert the person, the more suitable in one respect the person is for the role. However, now the employer will be thinking about suitability in a multi-faceted way. A number of aspects of the role will be under consideration, and the person may be thought to fit well to some but less well to others. There will be a profile of fit to the role to be evaluated and compared with other candidates. The personality profile will not provide information about all the aspects of the role but may provide information about a number.

Figure 4: Example of a candidate's job suitability profile

ASPECT OF ROLE	HOW IS IT ASSESSED?	RATING OF SUITABILITY (1 = highly unsuitable; 5 = highly suitable)
Communication skills	Interview	3
Developing relationships	Personality questionnaire	4
Team working	Personality questionnaire	3
Relevant experience	Interview + references	2
Flexibility	Interview + personality questionnaire	4
Problem solving	Interview + exercise	3
Computer skills	Interview + exercise	2

Another way of using personality questionnaires at this stage of selection is to review qualitatively what the person's personality profile implies. For this purpose an experienced interpreter of profiles will provide a written or verbal report based on the individual's profile. Alternatively, a computer-generated report may be used. These are profile interpretations generated automatically using complex expert systems that encapsulate the interpretative skills of a test expert.

Typically, the report will relate to both the strengths and weaknesses of the individual against the job requirements, but it will also provide a flavour of how the person might go about different types of task. The employer does not have a particular personality profile in mind but wants to consider how this person might function in the role and fit in to the organizational culture. In this case, the whole personality profile is considered. This interpretation of the profile will often raise some queries about how the individual will perform in the role, and these are noted down to be explored further at interview. In addition, the employer may want to confirm the results of the questionnaire through a discussion with the candidate. This will check whether the experiences the candidate describes at interview match the behavioural style that the personality questionnaire suggests. For instance, if the personality results suggest a person who is a slow and careful decision maker the employer might ask the candidate to talk about a recent important decision they have taken and consider whether the two accounts are consistent.

The nature of the role will determine how the employer will relate to a particular result and what aspects of the profile they will concentrate on. For a sales role, for example, the aspects of the personality profile that are relevant to relating to people and developing relationships will be one focus. For an administrative role, on the other hand, the information about the degree of structure in the working style is likely to be more relevant.

Example personality profile and report

Below is the example of a personality profile we looked at earlier. It is followed by a possible interpretation report based on these results.

Again, it should be remembered that only an outline of the traits measured by the questionnaire has been presented. In real life the actual results and the interpretation would depend on exactly what had been measured and in what detail.

Figure 5: Jay's personality profile and report

Unstructured			<>	Structured
Introvert		<>		Extrovert
Down to earth			<>	Imaginative
Independent		<>		Sympathetic
Anxious	<>			Relaxed

Interpretation of Jay's personality profile

Jay has completed the 'example' personality questionnaire. This is a broad measure of personality with five scales. Jay's results have been compared to a large group of job applicants and incumbents representative of the UK population.

He has described himself as someone who has quite a structured approach to his work. He is likely to prefer to plan and organize his work before starting. He will prefer to work in an environment where there are clear procedures and will follow these wherever possible and expect others to do the same. He has described himself as having a good eye for detail and as someone who is concerned to produce high-quality work to deadlines. This strong need for planning and structure may mean that he finds it difficult to change plans at the last minute or respond flexibly in a crisis. He may find it difficult to work with others who are less organized than he is.

Jay is someone who enjoys new experiences and is curious about the world. It is likely that he will enjoy learning and developing new skills. He has described himself as being imaginative and may tend to concentrate on ideas at the expense of the practical side of things. However, his creative thinking style may help him in problem solving and finding innovative approaches to his work. In addition, his organized approach is likely to help keep him grounded and maintain his focus on what needs to be done.

In terms of his relationship with others he has described himself as moderately extrovert, meaning that he does have some need to interact with others and is capable of developing good social skills if he does not already have them. His responses suggest that although he is not exceptionally lively he will be happy meeting new people and should be reasonably comfortable developing new relationships. However, he will also be tolerant of times when it is necessary to work with little interaction with others provided this is not constantly the case.

He has described himself as someone who balances the needs of others with his own need for autonomy. He is as sympathetic as the next person and is likely to be willing to help when others have problems. He should be able to work well in a team and be amenable and willing to compromise to meet team goals. However, he is likely to speak up when he feels strongly on a topic, and in these cases will not always be swayed from his own ideas to follow the group consensus.

His profile suggests that he is quite an anxious person. This may express itself in terms of general worries about work and other aspects of his life. His anxiety may also be a source of nervous energy for him. He may find that getting on with his work, checking for errors or making sure that details are correct helps allay his fears about potential problems or failure. He may become quite nervous before important events, such as presenting in front of a meeting. As someone who likes structure in his work, he may find that having clear instructions and procedures helps him keep calm. His anxiety may also show itself at times of crisis when the usual procedures may need to be abandoned and a new approach found.

Overall, the profile suggests that Jay is someone who would work well in a structured environment but who is likely to prefer to work where there is some variety or opportunity for some creativity in working or problem solving. He is likely to be moderately good at developing and maintaining relationships, and his organized approach may make him a good team member. Of some concern is his anxiety level, which is quite high, and it would be useful to explore how well he copes with stress and in an emergency.

Relating personality profiles to jobs

The way an employer might relate to the information provided in Jay's profile (see above) would depend on the job requirements in question. His profile is suitable for a typical administrative or clerical role, and he might also be well suited to work in a general call centre. However, he would be less suited to working in highly stressful environments, such as those in emergency services, or in those that required a lot of flexibility, such as a travel representative. While the profile contains a mix of positive and negative statements about Jay, the employer will focus on the statements most relevant to the role in question. If this leaves mainly negative statements it suggests that Jay would be unsuitable. If it left mainly positive statements Jay is more likely to be suited to the role.

In making decisions the employer would look at a variety of information about a candidate. Although personality is important, it is never the sole criterion for selection. The person's skills and abilities are usually considered first, and experience is also often an important factor. After these comes the way a person approaches their work, and personality questionnaires are one source of information on this, but they will be supplemented, generally with an interview and often with other exercises as well. The personality profile is only one part of the jigsaw.

Recruiters will be trying to understand the implications of all the information collected and will be particularly concerned about inconsistencies across the different sources of information. If a candidate says at interview that he managed a team of five people in his previous job, but the reference from his employer suggests he was only a team member and didn't formally manage anyone, this would undermine the candidate's credibility. In the same way, if the personality profile suggests an outgoing, fun-loving person but at interview the candidate is quite shy and describes preferring to work alone than in a team, this apparent contradiction will worry the interviewer. This is one of the reasons why the best strategy is to answer questionnaires as honestly as possible.

If a questionnaire is being used as part of a development process it may be used in a similar manner to the later stages of selection – that is, relating the person's personality style to the job requirements. The questionnaire results will often be related to a more general competency model. In particular, development processes usually want to identify a person's strengths and development needs. A personality questionnaire can help identify strengths that are not being exploited in the current role. These might suggest the direction of the next career move. An IT specialist who had good interpersonal skills could think about moving into management or training, for example. Where development needs are identified these can be addressed through an appropriate programme of activities. For instance, a customer service operative in a call centre who was high on agreeableness and struggled to deal with difficult clients might consider participating in some assertiveness training.

6 Completing a questionnaire

If you are asked to complete a personality questionnaire as part of a job application process there is less that you can do to prepare yourself than for other types of assessment. The questionnaire is just a structured way for you to describe yourself and your typical approach to work to the employer. This section reviews things you might like to do before you have to complete the questionnaire, discusses the best way to approach completing it and how to get the most out of completing a questionnaire.

Mode of presentation

There are a number of ways of completing a personality questionnaire. Often the questionnaire is presented in a paper format. These days, however, you might be asked to complete a questionnaire on computer or on a personal organizer. Whatever the format, you should be given clear instructions on what you have to do, and you should follow these carefully.

Paper questionnaires may be presented on a single sheet or in a booklet with many pages. You may be asked to mark your responses next to the question, but it is more likely that there will be a separate answer sheet for you to mark your responses on. Check that you have understood how you are expected to complete the answer sheet. Ask the administrator if you are not sure what to do.

Answer sheets are often read automatically by an optical reader, which is very accurate but will give an erroneous reading if you have not followed the instructions carefully. For instance, if you mark outside the designated area your response might not be picked up or may be misinterpreted. If you are asked to complete the questionnaire in pencil or black ink you must do so. The machine may not pick up marks in other colours as effectively. If you think you have made an error in completing the form tell the administrator and they will tell you what to do. You might, for example, be given an additional answer sheet and asked to copy your answers correctly.

If the questionnaire is presented in an electronic medium there should be full instructions on how to use the technology and how you should indicate your answers. The system should be straightforward enough for people who are not experienced in using a computer. Again, make sure you understand what you have to do, how you should indicate your answers and how you can change an answer if you wish to do so. Computer-based systems often have 'help' screens, which give further explanations if you need them or allow you to go back to the instructions to check something.

Preparation ahead of time

Most employers will provide you with information about what to expect during the selection process, and this will include whether a personality questionnaire is part of the process. It is generally considered good practice to provide candidates with clear information about a selection process, but because there is no specific preparation needed for completing a questionnaire, it may not be mentioned in advance.

The only skills you need to complete a personality questionnaire are the ability to read the questions and a knowledge of yourself and how you behave, think and feel. There is, therefore, no real need to do any preparation. Each of us is an expert on ourselves: we know what we like and don't like, what makes us happy and what makes us angry. You are not required to describe this in words, which might take some preparation, but just to answer a series of questions about yourself.

If, even so, you feel you would like to prepare you could try some of the following:

- Look at the example questions in Chapter 3 and think about how you would answer them. This will help you get used to responding to questions about yourself. You will find that you will sometimes need to generalize. We all behave in different ways in different situations – even the brightest optimist may sometimes expect things to go wrong. However, there is a general trend in behaviour, and this is what you should be using to guide your responses.

- Think about what sort of person you are and how this affects the way you work. Consider different work situations and how you respond to them. What kinds of situations and responses are you comfortable with? What sort of things do you find more difficult or awkward? Are you better working with a team or working alone? Do you prefer well-defined structured tasks or would you rather have a less well-defined role where you can make your own decisions on what you should and will do?

- Read through the descriptions of different personality traits in Chapter 4 and answer the questions at the end of each section. Think about which description suits you best. This will help you develop some insight into your own behavioural style and may help you answer questions more easily. Remember that your behaviour will differ from time to time and from situation to situation. Think about what is most typical for you, what you are most likely to do or what you would feel most comfortable doing.

- Check your thoughts about yourself with someone who knows you well. A good friend or a family member may be aware of how you usually respond to situations, even if you find it difficult to say. If the person you consult sees you differently, try asking them to answer the questions at the end of the section on behavioural style about you. If you do not agree on the answers discuss this with the person to try to understand what you are really like.

- Avoid over-analysing yourself. If you generally spend a lot of time analysing your behaviour and thinking about how you feel about things, you may find it easier to answer questionnaires if you don't focus on things in so much detail. Most questions are quite straightforward and do not require a great deal of self-analysis to answer.
- Collect what information you can about the role and the organization. The employer's website may be a good source of information about the culture of the organization. If you know someone who works for the same employer or in a similar type of job, ask them to tell you about what they do. Use this information to decide how your personal style might fit the role.

Completing a questionnaire at the employer's premises

If you are invited to attend a selection day but have not been provided with information about what it will entail, it is appropriate to contact the employer for more information. However, it may be the employer's policy not to give out such information or they may believe telling one candidate something that is not shared with all candidates would be unfair. Although you may feel the lack of information reflects poorly on the employer's processes it is probably not a good idea to press the point, because this may be seen negatively by the employer and reflect poorly on you throughout the selection process.

If you do know you have to complete a questionnaire there are a few important practical steps you should take. If you need glasses or contact lenses to be able to read clearly make sure you have these with you. Some people prefer not to wear glasses in public, but the danger of misunderstanding the questionnaire through poor vision is much more serious than any impact on your image of wearing glasses.

Plan how you will get to the venue in good time. Work out your route, find out the relevant transport options, look up timetables and so on. Employers will often send a map and details of how to get to their premises. Apart from the fact that arriving late is likely to create a poor impression, it can put you at a disadvantage in other ways. The employer may be working to a strict timetable and trying to see a number of candidates, and someone who is late can put the schedule out. You could find your interview time is shortened and you have less opportunity to impress the employer with your skills and abilities. If you are late, other applicants may already have started to complete questionnaires and tests, and it could be difficult to accommodate you.

You should also think of the impact on yourself of having to rush. You could arrive feeling hot and bothered, and if there is no time to calm down, you might end up having to complete the questionnaire, be interviewed or take part in another type of exercise while you are feeling flustered. This is likely to affect your concentration and therefore your performance. It is better to arrive too early and have to hang around for a bit than to rush in at the last minute.

Completing a questionnaire on your own

It is quite common now to be asked to complete a questionnaire in your own time before you attend for an interview with the employer, and some employers may send you a questionnaire in the post to complete. Usually, however, if you are asked to complete the questionnaire before the interview, you will be asked to do so on the internet. Typically, the employer will send you an e-mail with a link to a secure website where you can complete the questionnaire. You will usually be sent a username and password to ensure the security of the system.

If you are asked to complete a questionnaire on-line consider when and where you will do this and make sure that you set aside sufficient time to complete it. You should be told in advance about how long it will take, and it is important that you give yourself the best chance of completing it effectively. This means finding a quiet place where you will not be interrupted. If you have a computer at home this may be the best option. If you can, shut yourself away in a quiet room to complete the questionnaire, and warn the other people that live with you that you do not want to be interrupted. Switch off your mobile phone, music players, radios and TV, and if you can, switch off or unplug other phones. Alternatively, get someone else to answer the phone or let it go to answer phone.

Choose a time when you are feeling alert and ready to concentrate. It may be tempting to complete the exercise late at night or after you return from a night out, but think whether you are at your best. If you are tired or have been drinking, you may misread some of the questions or respond inappropriately. Make sure that you are seated comfortably. Get yourself a cup of coffee or tea or a cold drink if this helps you relax, but avoid alcohol or other drugs, which will alter the way you perceive yourself and could affect your responses.

If you do not have your own computer or internet connection at home or if the computer is located in a busy part of the house, think about an alternative place where you can use a computer in a quieter location. You may be able to use a computer at your place of work if you can find a quiet place. You will need to think about the appropriateness of using your employer's equipment to complete a questionnaire as part of an application for a job somewhere else. If you are applying for promotion in your own organization or if you are being made redundant, your employer might be happy for you to use the organization's facilities. Otherwise, it is unlikely to be appropriate.

Other places where you can access internet facilities include internet cafés, libraries and, if you are a student, colleges and universities. If you need to complete a questionnaire in one of these places consider the following:

- Find a quiet corner to work rather than somewhere where people are talking or constantly moving around. Certain times of day might be quieter and more conducive to completing a questionnaire.
- Make sure that the time you are allowed to use the machine is sufficient for completing the questionnaire. Libraries and colleges sometimes limit the length of internet sessions. Check if you are likely to be cut off in the middle. If necessary, explain

why you need a longer time to an administrator to see if they can help. If you are buying computer time at an internet café make sure that you have enough to finish the questionnaire.

- Switch off your mobile phone so you are not interrupted while you are completing the questionnaire.
- If you have not used a particular place before you may like to check it out in advance to make sure it is suitable.

Try to complete the questionnaire well ahead of any set deadline. If you leave it to the last minute and you encounter problems, there may not be time to sort them out. Although most systems are robust, you might encounter problems connecting to the site for the questionnaire or you might have difficulties with your username or password. Equally, your own computer equipment could just choose that moment to be temperamental. If the deadline is looming there may not be enough time to find somewhere else to complete the questionnaire.

You will usually be given details of a helpdesk or person to contact in case of difficulty. Do take advantage of this service if you have a problem. Remember, however, that it may not operate a 24-hour, seven-day service. Try to start completing the questionnaire early enough so that there is time to get help if you need it.

Similar considerations are important if you are completing a questionnaire on paper. Find a quiet, comfortable place to do it, and make sure you will not be interrupted while you are completing it. Allow sufficient time, and if you have been asked to post your responses back, make sure you send the questionnaire off in good time in case there is a problem with the post. If you want to be sure, take a copy of your responses in case the original gets lost in the post.

Completing the questionnaire

First, read the instructions carefully. Check that you have understood what you have been asked to do. On a 1–5 scale is 1 'Strongly agree' or 'Strongly disagree'? You also need to read the questions or statements with care. It is easy to misread a word. People often fail to notice a negative word such as 'no' or 'not' in a statement and respond in the opposite direction. Consider the following statements:

I make no mistakes in my work.
I make mistakes in my work.
I like meeting new people.
I dislike meeting new people.
I rarely come to work on time.
I usually come to work on time.

A careless reader might miss the 'no' in the first statement and answer as if it was the second, giving an erroneous picture of themselves. Similar errors are possible with the other pairs of statements.

You also need to make sure that you are indicating your responses according to the instructions. A frequent source of error with paper answer sheets is to respond to a question on the wrong line of the answer sheet. You may be answering Question 35 but mark your response against Question 36. This will lead you to mark your next answer incorrectly, that is marking the answer to Question 36 against the next empty line, which is the one for Question 37. Check that you are answering against the appropriate question number as you are completing the questionnaire to avoid this. If you find you have gone wrong, go back and change your answers. Check the instructions to see how changes to answers should be marked. Should you erase it or cross it out? If you find you have been marking against the wrong number for a long time ask the administrator what you should do. You may be given a new answer sheet and asked to copy your answers across correctly.

When you are answering a questionnaire you are providing a description of yourself and how you typically behave and react to things. The questions just help you structure this and describe the aspects of your personality in which the employer is interested. There are no right or wrong answers to the questions. Rather, each person's answer should reflect their personality. Therefore, you should think about yourself in relation to the question or statement. Is it describing something you often do or something you rarely do? Does the word describe you well or not?

It is important to answer all the questions, even if you are not sure how to respond to some of them. Your score on the questionnaire will be distorted if you don't answer some of the questions. If you are responding on a computer it may not let you send your responses until you have answered all the questions. An administrator will check your paper answer sheet to make sure you have answered all the questions and ask you to go back and complete any you have skipped.

The majority of questions in questionnaires are quite straightforward, and it should be clear what is being asked, because questionnaire developers try to make the content easy to understand. However, you might find some questions ambiguous and not be quite sure what is intended. Do not worry about this if it is just the occasional question. Make your best guess at what is intended and answer accordingly. If you are finding it difficult to understand many of the questions, check the instructions to make sure you have understood correctly what you need to do.

Always try to answer questions honestly. This will provide the employer with the most accurate picture of you as a person to see how well you would fit into the job and the organization. By describing yourself as you are, you give a true impression of yourself. If you believe you are suitable for the role, this should come across in your responses. Don't worry about providing the odd response that may seem quite negative. The employer will be looking at the totality of your responses rather than the answers to specific questions.

Don't try to guess what the employer is looking for. This can make responding difficult, and it is, in any case, unlikely to help you make a good impression for a number of reasons. First, you may be wrong and make yourself look unsuitable for the job when you are, in fact, exactly what the employer is looking for. It is difficult to predict what sort of responses an employer might be looking for, so you could be giving exactly the wrong impression. Second, questionnaires often contain checks on response patterns, and these can flag up inconsistent or unusual answers. Third, if you distort your answers you cannot be sure what impression you are creating. Last, the employer may want to discuss your results with you and contradictions between your profile and what you say at interview will become evident and be potentially embarrassing.

Some people do find it difficult to respond to questionnaires and agonize about what to say. They can think of times when the statement applies to them and times when it does not, or they agree with part of the statement and not with another part. If you are having difficulty responding to a question try the suggestions below.

Hints on answering questions

Answer quickly instead of thinking at length over a question. Your first response is likely to be your best answer and the one that reflects you most accurately. Brooding over a question may be what is leading to the confusion by raising too many possibilities. Questionnaires do not have fixed time limits, but it is better to work at a good pace than to spend a lot of time over individual questions.

Think about the question in a work-related context. What is important is how you behave at work. If the way you are at home with friends and family is different from the way you are at work, consider how you would behave on a typical work day.

If you do not have a job at the moment, think about previous jobs you have had. If you have never worked or if the jobs you have had are not really relevant, think about yourself in work-like situations. This might include studying in school, college or university, doing voluntary work for a charity or even completing tasks at home like housework. If you have a hobby that you spend time on or have worked with friends to organize an event, you can use this experience to think about how you behave when responding to questions.

Consider what you know about the organization or the job itself. This can narrow down the range of experience you need to think about. Does thinking about the question in this context help you decide how to answer?

Try to rule out some options so that you have fewer to choose from. For instance if you have to answer the following question:

I finish one task before moving onto the next.
a. Strongly agree
b. Agree

c. Neither agree nor disagree

d. Disagree

e. Strongly disagree

First, think whether you generally agree or generally disagree. For instance, if you decide that you generally disagree you can rule out options a, b and c. Now you need to decide between d and e. Is this something that you never do, option e, or do you sometimes finish things before moving on, option d? Alternatively, if you can't decide whether you agree or disagree then you can rule out options a and e. Now think whether you are more likely to finish something before moving on, or more likely to move on immediately. Think about this in a work situation. Bring to mind a few occasions recently when you had to start a new task. Had you finished the previous one? Can you see a trend? If you still can't see a trend then choose option c and move on.

Here is another example of a different type of question.

Select the word that **most** describes you and the one that **least** describes you.

	MOST LIKE ME	LEAST LIKE ME
Creative		
Practical		
Helpful		
Obedient		

First, think of what is most like you. Can you rule out any words that are not like you at all? Now consider the words left and compare them in pairs. For instance, are you more creative or more practical? It is often easier to decide between a pair of words than a whole list. Think about a work situation where you could choose between doing something creative, such as thinking up ideas to improve the way you work, or something practical, such as getting on with a task. If you are more practical than creative then creative is not most like you. Now compare practical with the next remaining option. Are you more practical or more helpful? If you find one of the pairs difficult to decide between leave it and go on to the next one. So if you can't decide about practical and helpful, compare practical and obedient. Suppose you feel you are more obedient. Now you need to compare obedient and helpful. Which is more like you? If you still can't decide between the last two words you can just choose one at random. You have already ruled out two words, so this is more than just a guess. Now you can do the same thing with the remaining words to find which one is least like you.

If you have a disability

Despite the protection of the Disability Discrimination Act, disabled people may still face discrimination from employers who overestimate the impact of the disability or feel that a disabled employee will be a burden. For this reason people with disabilities do not always want to disclose their disability to an employer early on in the selection process, and there is no requirement for them to do so. If there is any concern that the employer is not disability friendly, not disclosing is a sensible approach. Some disabilities are readily visible and will become evident as soon as you turn up to interview, but most are not and can remain hidden. However, if there is anything about your disability that could affect your performance at interview it is usually worthwhile to let an employer know. This will trigger your rights to adjustments and accommodations under the law.

If you have any kind of disability that could affect your ability to complete a questionnaire you should let the employer know. This might include visual impairments of various kinds, dyslexia, difficulties in concentration or motor difficulties that affect writing or using a computer. It is a requirement of the Disability Discrimination Act that employers make reasonable adjustments to selection procedures to allow candidates with a disability to take part without being put at a disadvantage.

If you have a disability and have not received any information from the employer about the nature of the selection procedure, do contact them to check whether there will be anything in the selection process that might cause you difficulties. If you prefer this can be done without revealing your disability status: just ask if there will be any need to read or write during the selection day. However, if you do need some accommodation, you will need to reveal your disability to claim your rights. Employers are not required to make adjustments if they do not know about your disability. Even if you have ticked the box on the application form to say you have a disability, this is not sufficient to trigger an adjustment. The employer will still need further information to know if your disability is one that needs an adjustment or accommodation and, if so, what changes are needed.

The more information and the more notice you give the employer, the more you can expect to be done to accommodate you. For example, if you need quite a large font size to be able to read, you will need to let the employer know your needs in sufficient time for them to arrange to have an appropriate version of the questionnaire available. If you only mention this need on the day when you arrive, the employer will probably not have a suitable format available for you and you may have to struggle with an ordinary version. Employment tribunals do not expect employer's to make adjustments if they have not been notified with details of a person's disability and needs. If the notification is at the last minute they will not expect employers to do as much as they could with proper notice.

If you feel that an employer has not made an appropriate adjustment for you or has discriminated against you in the selection process you can contact the Commission for Equality and Human Rights (www.cehr.org.uk) for advice and help in taking things further. Until 2008 providing this help is the responsibility of the Disability Rights Commission (www.drc-gb.org); thereafter it will be merged into the Commission for Equality and Human Rights.

If English is not your primary language

Questionnaires used in Britain are designed for use with people whose primary language is English. If English is not your first language consider whether you know enough English to understand and answer the questionnaire. Remember that questions may contain local idioms and metaphors. Look at the example questions in Chapter 4 to see if you can understand them easily. If you think your command of English may not be good enough to allow you to properly understand the questionnaire get in touch with the employer to discuss this problem. It may be possible to provide the questionnaire in other languages or to provide you with some help – a dictionary for example – so that you can complete the questionnaire in English.

After completing the questionnaire

After completing the questionnaire the employer will arrange for it to be scored. The results will be used alongside other information in making decisions about you. Depending on the stage in the selection process and the selection process itself, the employer may want to talk to you about your results, but this will not always happen. Many employers will not consider the results of the personality questionnaire at the interview but treat them separately. Employers who want to explore your results further may devote a whole interview to discussing them with you, but many will integrate a few specific points from your personality results into a general interview

The main purpose of an interview about the results of your personality questionnaire is to better understand your suitability for the job. The employer might have a few questions arising from your personality profile about your strengths and weakness in terms of the job requirements and want to explore these further with you. In addition, the employer will want to see if your behaviour at interview matches your personality profile.

If the employer wants to have this sort of discussion with you, you should prepare as you would for any other interview. Think about how well your approach and style would suit the job you are applying for. What are your strengths in this regard? Where are you likely to be particularly well suited? Think of some examples of how your personality style has helped you in other jobs or work-like situations. For instance, if you have a particularly organized approach, how has this helped you in your work? Has it made you more efficient and effective? Similarly, if you tend to do things spontaneously rather than in an organized way think about how this has helped you in your work. Has it made you more flexible and able to deal with unexpected situations?

You also need to think through areas where you have less fit to the job requirements and any aspects of your personality that might concern the employer. How will you make sure that this will not affect your performance? Try to think of occasions when you have shown that you can be effective despite a particular aspect of your personality. Suppose the job requires a person who is quite organized. If you have a tendency to be disorganized, does this mean you have a tendency to miss details or fail to meet deadlines? Can you show how you have overcome this in previous work? What is your track record in meeting important deadlines? Have you learned tools and techniques that help you to be more organized when this is important? Of course, if you really find it difficult to work in an organized manner, perhaps this role is not suitable for you and you should look for a job where this trait is not so important.

Not all jobs require an organized approach. For some work it is more important to be flexible and adapt to changing circumstances than to follow plans and have a structured approach. If you tend to be very structured in your approach how do you manage when circumstances change and you need to adapt or when you have to work in rather disorganized surroundings? If you would really hate working in this kind of environment, a job that requires it is probably not for you, but if you think you would like the job nevertheless, think how you would cope with a workplace that may be disorderly and constantly in flux. Can you think of an example when you have faced this kind of situation and coped well? Do you have strategies and techniques for dealing with this kind of situation? How would you persuade an employer that, despite your natural tendencies, you would be effective in the muddle surrounding you?

Do not feel downcast because the personality questionnaire might have revealed some areas where you have a less good fit to the job requirements than others. The employer will be looking for a variety of things from candidates. As well as some aspects of personal style and fit with the organization, there will be skills, abilities, knowledge and experience. It is rare to meet a candidate who fits the job requirements perfectly. Most candidates have some areas of good match against the required specification and some areas of poor match. The purpose of the selection process is to find out about the candidate's match to the job requirements. In making a decision the employer will be balancing the different sets of strengths and weaknesses of the various candidates, and they might have to decide between someone who had exactly the right sort of experience but a poor attitude to work and someone who had very little experience but seemed exactly the sort of person to fit in to the organization. If you can show how you can overcome areas where your match is less than perfect you still have a good chance of being successful.

Requesting feedback

Even if the employer does not want to discuss your personality questionnaire results with you as part of the selection process you may be offered feedback on your results separately. It is considered good practice for employers to offer feedback whenever they use psychometric testing. Feedback may be offered in a number of ways. You may be provided with a written report about your results, the employer may give a telephone number you can call to receive feedback from someone, or you may be able to receive feedback face to face, either during the interview or at another time during the assessment day. Successful candidates may be able to receive feedback after they start work. An example of what a feedback report might look like is included in Chapter 5.

If you are offered the opportunity it is worth taking it up because you can use feedback from a personality questionnaire as a development opportunity. People pay substantial fees to have their personality profiled and to receive feedback, and you have the opportunity to do this at no cost to yourself. There are a number of benefits from receiving feedback on your results. First, you may find the feedback interesting in itself. In one sense the personality questionnaire should not tell you anything you don't know about yourself – it is based on the information you provided about yourself through your responses – but the way the information is organized and presented may give you a perspective on yourself and your behaviour that provides you with a new insight about yourself.

In addition to your understanding of yourself, the feedback report may also help you appreciate how you might be seen by other people, particularly prospective employers. The report might include some of the implications of your behavioural style for how you work, and you should use this information to consider how you might present yourself more effectively for jobs. The information can also help you appreciate what types of jobs and organizations you might be most suited to. Think about where your personality style contributes positively to your performance but also where it might sometimes obstruct you in doing your job. What could you do to get round the difficulty? How could you show a new employer that you can cope well with the situations and tasks that suit you less well? How can you present your strengths most effectively?

Your personality profile also has implications for how you approach being a job applicant, how you respond at interview and whether you find the process difficult or exciting. Chapter 4 discussed the implications of some personality traits for behaviour as a job candidate. You might be able to use the information about your own personality profile to understand your strengths and development needs for the role of job candidate. If there are areas where you behavioural style is detracting from your effectiveness in selling yourself, you could look at ways of developing a better approach. For example, introverts could practise singing their own praises, and people low on emotional stability could look at stress-management techniques.

You can also use the feedback to think about your own development more generally. Remember that there are no right or wrong personalities, and it is not that one person has a better personality than another. Rather, it is a matter of the suitability of a behavioural style for a particular field of performance. You can use your personality feedback to think about your behavioural style and how you can use it to best advantage. Are there aspects of your personality that you do not have the opportunity to express in your current line of work? Are there requirements of your current work that your personality makes you less comfortable with? Someone who was quite unsociable and disliked interacting with people would be less comfortable with a job that required a lot of team work or working with people in other ways. An example of a personality trait making a role less convivial for someone might be a computer technician with low sociability whose role included training people to use their computers and providing support when there were computer problems. Such a person might find it quite draining having to work with people a lot of the time and prefer a role where there was more technical work with machines and less with people. On the other hand, an example of an unused personality trait might be a more sociable and friendly computer technician who finds their people skills are little used as they spend all day working with machines.

If you are not offered feedback you can always ask to see if it is available. Even if the employer is not able to provide feedback, you may encourage them to offer it next time. If the results of your personality questionnaire are held on computer or in a filing system you can request the results using a data access request under the Data Protection Act. The requirement is to provide you with a meaningful explanation of the data held on you, which in this case would be an interpretation of your personality profile. Employers can ask you to pay up to £10 for the results of a data access request. See the Information Commissioner's website for more details (www.ico.gov.uk).

Standards in the use of questionnaires

Personality questionnaires, like other psychometric instruments, are complex tools, which are difficult to create and should be used only by people who have appropriate training and skills. There are no legal constraints on publishing or using tests, but there are standards and guidelines that define a generally agreed benchmark of good practice.

A great deal of work goes into developing an effective test or questionnaire. A multi-stage iterative process is usually used in developing tests. First, it is important to develop questions that assess the appropriate personality traits. These are then subjected to detailed review and trialling on large groups of people. Comprehensive statistical analyses are performed to understand how well the questionnaires are working. Following this, the test is revised, and the reviews, trials and statistical analysis are repeated until the test can be seen to be fair and effective. It is difficult for an untrained person to assess the quality of a questionnaire, but the British Psychological Society publishes a register of tests that have been certified to reach a minimum quality standard. This can be accessed on the British Psychological Society Psychological Testing Centre website (www.psychtesting.org.uk). You can use this site to check if the test you have completed was registered; alternatively you can call on 0116252 9530. Because a test has not been registered does not mean it is a poor instrument, but reputable test publishers generally submit their tests and questionnaires for registration and review.

Questionnaires should not ask inappropriately intrusive questions or questions on topics that are not relevant to the world of work. Questions about your sexual fantasies, religious beliefs or childhood relationships should not be used in a personality questionnaire for standard occupational use. The questions should cover topics that you would feel comfortable talking about to a colleague at work. The individual questions are designed to sample your behaviour in a particular domain, and the specific content of each question is not of any particular relevance except as an example of the trait being measured. The employer will not be looking at your individual responses to questions but at the collated responses from a group of questions.

Employers should notify you that you will be asked to complete a test or questionnaire in advance. They should explain to you how and why the test is being used and what they will be doing with the scores. You should understand who will have access to your results and what will happen to them after the selection procedure is complete, whether you are successful or not. This should include a commitment to maintain the confidentiality of your results. They should also let you know how you can have access to your results.

Although there is no requirement to do so, it is considered good practice to provide test-takers with feedback on their results. This can be in the form of a written or oral report. If a written report is provided, candidates should be given contact details for a person who can help with any queries they may have about the report.

Test users should be trained in using tests and questionnaires. The training covers topics such as test selection, test administration and test interpretation. Reputable test publishers require proof of training to use tests before they will sell their instruments, and the British Psychological Society runs an accreditation scheme for test training. People who interpret personality questionnaires should have at least an Intermediate Level B Certificate of Competence. Test administrators require a lower level of qualification, a Test Administrators' certificate. Again, this scheme is not mandatory, but you can check at the British Psychological Society Psychological Testing Centre website (www.psychtesting.org.uk) if the person interpreting your test is on the register. Individual test publishers also hold more comprehensive registers, but only of the people qualified to use their tests and questionnaires.

If you feel you have not been treated properly and fairly by an employer in their use of tests and questionnaires you should complain to the employer in the first instance. They are often concerned that applicants should feel they were assessed fairly – especially when applicants may also be potential customers. As an applicant, however, you have very few legal rights. You can choose to withdraw, of course, but there is little employment law that has reference to the selection process. If you feel you have been treated unfairly because of your race, gender, age, religion, sexual orientation or because of a disability you can make a claim through an employment tribunal. (See www.employmenttribunals.gov.uk or www.acas.org.uk for more information or contact the Commission for Equality and Human Rights, www.cehr.org.uk.)

If you feel that the way the questionnaire was used was inappropriate you can contact the publisher. Most test publishers are concerned that their instruments are used properly, and they will sell questionnaires only to people who have had appropriate training. The test publisher may be able to tell you if the treatment you received was appropriate. In some cases they may wish to contact the employer to investigate further, and test publishers will refuse to supply tests to people who misuse them. The British Psychological Society will follow up any complaints about psychologists who are members of the society. However, it has little jurisdiction over people who have certificates of competence in testing who are not psychologists.

If you have been assessed internally within your organization for development purposes or other reasons and you feel your treatment was inappropriate you can use your company's grievance procedure to raise any issues if an informal approach to the people responsible for the assessment is unsatisfactory. You can also contact your trade union representative if appropriate. As an employee you have more rights than an applicant. For instance, if the outcome of an assessment procedure was that you are made redundant, you have the right to be treated reasonably by the employer and can take complaints to employment tribunals if they are serious.

As well as expecting an employer to treat you with respect and consideration during an assessment procedure, you should consider your own behaviour in the testing session. In particular you should:

- Treat others with respect and courtesy during the assessment process. This includes both the representatives of the employer and other candidates whom you meet.
- Follow the instructions of the test administrator.
- Take responsibility for your own performance. Listen carefully to instructions. If you do not understand what you have to do, ask the administrator before you begin.
- Tell an appropriate person about anything that might invalidate the questionnaire results or that you would wish to have taken into consideration.
- Engage constructively with the assessment process.

Frequently asked questions

In this section there are answers to some of the common questions people ask about questionnaires. They are answered in more detail elsewhere.

What am I revealing about myself when I fill in a questionnaire?
Questionnaires used in an employment context are designed to elicit information about how someone would approach their work and fit into the organization. By completing a questionnaire you are just describing what you are like as a person and providing the type of information that someone who knew you well at work might be able to provide. Questionnaires used for employment purposes are not designed to provide insights into your private thoughts and fantasies. You should not encounter clinical psychological assessments, which can be more intrusive.

Why are there so many questions in a test?
Questionnaires can be long, and some have hundreds of questions. Others are much shorter with perhaps a few tens of questions. There are a number of reasons for lengthy questionnaires. First, all things being equal, the longer the test the more accurate it is. Second, the more detailed the questionnaire the more aspects of personality it will assess, and it will therefore need more questions to make these finer distinctions. Third, the repeated inclusion of similar questions can be used to assess the consistency with which the questionnaire has been completed.

Why are some of the questions not relevant for the job I am applying for?
Because personality questionnaires are difficult and expensive to develop most employers use standard questionnaires, which they can buy from

test publishers, rather than developing a measure tailored to their needs. Typically, these questionnaires will have a mix of relevant and irrelevant content for the job in question.

How do I know if the questionnaire I am asked to complete is reputable?
It is difficult for someone who is not trained in the use of tests to evaluate the effectiveness of an instrument. Test publishers can submit their tests to be registered as meeting minimum quality standards for use by the British Psychological Society. They can also submit a test for a detailed review. Reputable publishers generally do this. You can check whether the test you have taken is registered and/or see a précis of the test review at the British Psychological Society Psychological Testing Centre website (www.psychtesting.org.uk).

Are tests fair?
Questionnaire developers generally invest a lot of work in making sure that their instruments are accurate measures and do not suffer from biases of any kind. In general, standardized objective measures are much less open to bias than other methods of assessment an employer might use. For instance, interviews are, by their nature, subjective, and the prejudices of the interviewer can affect the results. In the past test developers were much less aware of issues of fairness and bias, and some early tests and questionnaires did contain inappropriate content. These instruments have typically either fallen out of use or have been revised.

Why won't the employer tell me my actual score on a test?
Scores on tests and questionnaires are just numbers, and without an understanding of how these numbers are derived they are not meaningful. If you are told you scored 3 on a scale of a questionnaire this will not really help you understand what it means. Guidelines suggest that it is better to provide people with information about the meaning of their scores rather than the scores themselves.

Why won't the employer give me feedback on my results?
It is good practice to provide people who have completed tests and

questionnaires with some feedback on their results. This is becoming easier now that there are readily available computer-generated reports for most questionnaires. However, some employers do not do this because of the time required and the cost of providing the information when there are many candidates.

Are psychological questionnaires any better than horoscopes?
There is a great deal of objective research evidence to show that personality questionnaires can provide quite accurate information about people and that it is helpful in selecting the best candidates for jobs and supporting individual development. For example, studies on tens of thousands of people show that people with appropriate personality profiles perform better on jobs. There are also research studies that show that when people are provided with a standard report and told it is their own personalized personality profile they will often rate it as quite accurate. This shows that it is possible to create generalizations that many people find insightful. This could explain why many people find horoscopes quite persuasive, although there are hardly any employers who use this approach in selecting staff.

How do you interpret a questionnaire result?
This is a complex topic, and answering it is the main content of the training that people must undergo before they are allowed to use tests and questionnaires (see Chapter 5 for a fuller discussion). Most psycho-logical questionnaires are assessed by comparing the individual's response pattern to a known comparison group. This allows you to say whether the person has answered questions in a particular area, for instance, anxiety, in a more or less extreme manner than is typical of relevant others. It is possible to say whether people have described themselves as more anxious than 10 per cent of the population (so they have described themselves as quite relaxed and not very anxious) or more anxious than 90 per cent of the population (that is, they have described themselves as highly anxious). However, this is just the beginning of interpretation. The test user must go on to say what is the implication of this level of anxiety for the job – is it helpful to have a low, medium or high degree of anxiety in this role, or is anxiety not relevant to the role?

In addition, it is important to look at the level of anxiety together with the other facets measured by the questionnaire. For instance, how does the person's degree of structure interact with their degree of anxiety? Someone who is relaxed and unstructured may cope well with stressful situations but may be too laid back to get things done. Someone who is anxious and structured may be quite obsessively careful in their work. This can be very useful in safety-critical environments but can be an impediment where work needs to be delivered quickly. A shop assistant who takes hours lining up goods perfectly might be wasting time that could be used to encourage sales.

Isn't there a danger of cloning when employers use personality questionnaires?

If employers were to specify the exact profile they were looking for on a personality questionnaire for a particular job there would be a danger of cloning. However, this is not the way that questionnaires are used. First, for any job only part of the profile will be relevant. Second, while employers may be looking for scores in a particular range on a scale, this range will be quite broad and encompass a degree of variation within it. Third, employers will often take on people who do not exactly match the criteria they set because they have other desirable qualities – skills and experience, immediate availability – or because they fit the profile better than other candidates assessed. Finally, many employers look at profiles qualitatively rather than in a fixed way. They use the information to better understand how a candidate might perform in the role without having a specific view of what their preferred personality type for the role is.

How can I practise completing a test and get some feedback?

Although there is benefit to be gained from practising reasoning tests of various sorts, there is no need to practise completing a personality questionnaire. Chapter 6 describes things to do to prepare for a test, but the difficulty in taking a test for practice is that proper personality questionnaires are carefully conserved to prevent them from being overused, so easily available tests, such as those that can be accessed on the web, are of variable quality. However, if you would like to try a short questionnaire as an example, the following link will allow you to do this: www.bbc.co.uk/science, then search for personality. This questionnaire is a short questionnaire developed to be like the commonly used type questionnaires.

The University of Waterloo in Canada has a site for students that allows you to self-assess your personality motivation and interests, although it isn't quite like a standard questionnaire. See www.cdm.uwaterloo.ca/step1.asp. Some of the books in the Further Reading allow you to self-assess your personality in different ways.

Personality questionnaires prevent some people from getting jobs, don't they?

A personality questionnaire is just a tool to help employers collect information about a candidate. There are no good or bad profiles; it is a question of appropriateness to job requirements. It is the employer who decides, based on this information and other sources, whether the candidate is suitable. You should remember that an employer will typically see between two and ten candidates for every vacancy, and they may have many more applicants at the initial stages. This means that in the end most candidates will be rejected, no matter what selection method is used. Being rejected does not mean that you could not do the job. It simply means that the employer saw someone who, in their opinion, could do the job better than you. Often most of the candidates who apply for a job would be reasonably effective, and it is the nature of the selection process that many able people are rejected. If you are not having much success in applying for a job, try not to be too downhearted. It does not mean that you do not have potential. Always ask for feedback to try to understand why you have not been successful. Look for ways you can develop your skills and approach. At the same time, consider whether you are applying for the right sort of job and organization for you. There are many self-help materials to help you with a career search. See Further Reading for some suggestions.

How can I contact a test publisher?

The British Psychological Society Psychological Testing Centre website (www.psychtesting.org.uk) has a directory of test publishers with up-to-date contact details. The British Test Publishers Association also has a directory of members' contact details on their website (www.btpa.org).

Further reading

Listed are a range of books about testing and tests, personality, the recruitment and selection process as well as some self-development books.

More about personality questionnaires and profiles

Gifts Differing: Understanding Personality Type, Isabell Briggs Myers and Peter Myers (Davies Black Publishing, 1995)

The Psychologist's Book of Personality Tests: 24 Revealing Tests to Identify and Overcome Your Personal Barriers to a Better Life, Louis H. Janda (John Wiley & Sons Inc, 2001)

Testing People at Work: Competencies in Psychometric Testing, Mike Smith and Pam Smith (Blackwell Publishing, 2004)

Impact of personality on work performance

Team Roles at Work, Meredith Belbin (Butterworth-Heinemann Ltd, 2003)

Type Talk at Work: How the Sixteen Personality Types Determine Your Success on the Job, O. Kroeger, J. Thuesen and H. Rutledge (Delta, 2002)

Working with Emotional Intelligence, Daniel Goleman (Bloomsbury Publishing, 1999)

Career development aids

Build Your Own Rainbow: Workbook for Career and Life Management, Barrie Hopson and Mike Scally (Management Books, 1999)

Perfect Interview, Max Eggert (Random House, 2003)

The Seven Habits of Highly Effective People, Stephen R. Covey (Simon & Schuster, 1999)

The Work We were Born to Do: Find the Work You Love, Love the Work You Do, Nick Williams (Element Books, 2000)

What Color Is Your Parachute?: A Practical Guide for Job-Hunters and Career Changers: Workbook, Richard Bolles (Ten Speed Press, 2006)

Notes

Perfect Psychometric Test Results

Joanna Moutafi and Ian Newcombe

All you need to get it right first time

- Have you been asked to sit a psychometric test?
- Do you want guidance on the sorts of questions you'll be asked?
- Do you want to make sure you perform to the best of your abilities?

Perfect Psychometric Test Results is an essential guide for anyone who wants to secure their ideal job. Written by a team from Kenexa, one of the UK's leading compilers of psychometric tests, it explains how each test works, gives helpful pointers on how to get ready, and provides professionally constructed sample questions for you to try out at home. It also contains an in-depth section on online testing – the route that more and more recruiters are choosing to take. Whether you're a graduate looking to take the first step on the career ladder, or you're planning an all-important job change, *Perfect Psychometric Test Results* has everything you need to make sure you stand out from the competition.

BOOKS

Perfect Numerical Test Results

Joanna Moutafi and Ian Newcombe

All you need to get it right first time

- Have you been asked to sit a numerical reasoning test?
- Do you want guidance on the sorts of questions you'll be asked?
- Do you want to make sure you perform to the best of your abilities?

Perfect Numerical Test Results is an invaluable guide for anyone who wants to secure their ideal job. Written by a team from Kenexa, one of the UK's leading compilers of psychometric tests, it explains how numerical tests work, gives helpful pointers on how to get ready, and provides professionally constructed sample questions for you to try out at home. It also contains an in-depth section on online testing – the route that more and more recruiters are choosing to take. Whether you're a graduate looking to take the first step on the career ladder, or you're planning an all-important job change, *Perfect Numerical Test Results* has everything you need to make sure you stand out from the competition.

BOOKS

Perfect CV

Max Eggert

All you need to get it right first time

- Are you determined to succeed in your job search?
- Do you need guidance on how to make a great first impression?
- Do you want to make sure your CV stands out?

Bestselling *Perfect CV* is essential reading for anyone who's applying for jobs. Written by a leading HR professional with years of experience, it explains what recruiters are looking for, gives practical advice about how to show yourself in your best light, and provides real-life examples to help you improve your CV. Whether you're a graduate looking to take the first step on the career ladder, or you're planning an all-important job change, *Perfect CV* will help you stand out from the competition.

BOOKS

Perfect Interview

Max Eggert

All you need to get it right first time

- Are you determined to succeed in you job search?
- Do you want to make sure you have the edge on the other candidates?
- Do you want to find out what interviewers are *really* looking for?

Perfect Interview is an invaluable guide for anyone who's applying for jobs. Written by a leading HR professional with years of experience in the field, it explains how interviews are constructed, gives practical advice about how to show yourself in your best light, and provides real-life examples to help you practise at home. Whether you're a graduate looking to take the first step on the career ladder, or you're planning an all-important job change, *Perfect Interview* will help you stand out from the competition.

BOOKS

Order more titles in the *Perfect series*
from your local bookshop, or have them delivered
direct to your door by Bookpost.

Perfect Answers to Interview Questions	Max Eggert	9781905211722	£7.99
Perfect Babies' Names	Rosalind Fergusson	9781905211661	£5.99
Perfect Best Man	George Davidson	9781905211784	£5.99
Perfect CV	Max Eggert	9781905211739	£5.99
Perfect Interview	Max Eggert	9781905211746	£7.99
Perfect Numerical Test Results	Joanna Moutafi and Ian Newcombe	9781905211333	£7.99
Perfect Psychometric Test Results	Joanna Moutafi and Ian Newcombe	9781905211678	£7.99
Perfect Pub Quiz	David Pickering	9781905211692	£6.99
Perfect Punctuation	Stephen Curtis	9781905211685	£5.99
Perfect Readings for Weddings	Jonathan Law	9781905211098	£6.99
Perfect Wedding Speeches and Toasts	George Davidson	9781905211777	£5.99

Free post and packing
Overseas customers allow £2 per paperback

Phone: 01624 677237

Post: Random House Books
c/o Bookpost, PO Box 29, Douglas, Isle of Man IM99 1BQ
Fax: 01624 670 923

email: bookshop@enterprise.net

Cheques (payable to Bookpost) and credit cards accepted

Prices and availability subject to change without notice.
Allow 28 days for delivery.
When placing your order, please state if you do not wish to receive any
additional information.

www.randomhouse.co.uk